Servant Selling!

Three Keys to Selling Your Way To Significance And Success

1. Stewardship
2. Serving
3. Selling

O. Bernard Smalls

Table of Contents

Preface

In the mid 1970's I found myself in Anchorage, Alaska playing in a rhythm and blues funk band. After getting married, I knew I needed a more stable income. My skills were very limited at the time so I took a job washing cars in the National Car Rental detail department of Alaska Sales and Service, the largest General Motors dealership in Anchorage.

I quickly moved up to rental agent in the National Car Rental division and then office clerk, office assistant, and eventually office manager! WOW! As office manager, a part of my job was car control, which led to me helping sell the rental fleet when the rental vehicles had gone beyond the mileage limit. I found out that *I Loved Selling* and eventually moved in to sales as a commissioned sales person where I knew the Big Bucks were! I later found out that I had *the gift of gab* so I found myself teaching and training small pockets of interested sales people in sales. I had no formal sales training program at the time. I just taught them what worked for me. In January of 2000, I went through two weeks of intense training at the Blanchard Training and Development campus in Escondido, California, at the invitation of legendary business author, Dr. Ken Blanchard.

In November of 2000 I saw two trailers on the corner of what use to be solid woods near the then still under construction Mall of Georgia. I drove by it regularly and noticed a sign that said TOYOTA MALL OF GEORGIA opening soon. I thought, this is just five minutes from my house, close to Nordstrom and Starbucks! I feel the call to work here. To make a long story short, I was hired as one of the first pre-owned sales persons for the dealership. After being in sales for three months I was asked to become the corporate trainer. A primary responsibility as corporate trainer was training the sales team in what I called sales excellence. We won every excellence award Toyota has, making history in our first year of business.

Once while I was attending a seminar during the question and answer session a participant asked Peter Daniels, the millionaire Australian entrepreneur, who by the way endorsed my first book on customer service, "Mr. Daniels what would you do if you lost all of your wealth?" I was astonished by how quickly he responded by saying, "I would find something to sell, because commission is set for mediocrity and any fool can beat mediocrity!"

I hope you will read and understand **Servant Selling** and grasp the six fundamentals of selling your way to success and significance!

"Selling is simple, you just tell the truth attractively..."
Peter J. Daniels

Bernard Smalls
Summer 2005
Suwanee, Georgia

Dedication

This book is dedicated to all of the commissioned sales persons that have focused on selling their way out of debt and into significance and success. You are some of the most exceptional, yet under-rated people in our society. You are not a dime a dozen – ***You are shinning stars!***

Chapter 1

Servant Selling

Servant Selling may seem like an oxymoron in the competitive world that we live it but it is actually a sound concept that works. Most sales people see selling as a fight for the checkbook with the customer where the salesperson and customer are in an antagonistic relationship. This is the general attitude of most sales people that struggle from month to month for a paycheck. It does not have to be that way for you. I believe that you have picked up this book because of a deep conviction and desire to do it right and prosper in the world of professional selling.

The English word *"sell"* comes from a root word, which in the Scandinavian language means to *serve*. WOW!   That's revolutionary! To sell really means to serve. Customer service and selling are really synonymous terms when you look at it this way. Most organizations today emphasize selling as the major goal because that's how we get paid. We have all heard the saying; nothing happens until somebody sells something, and that's true to a degree. I submit to you that nothing happens until somebody serves someone. The goal of this book is to help you to see selling as serving and vice-versa. I guarantee you that if you will, you will see more financial profitability in sales. I love what Ken Blanchard says in his excellent book entitled Big Bucks! Profit is the applause we get for taking care of our customers. That is the basis for Servant Selling.

Servant Selling

SELLING IN THE 21st CENTURY

Selling in the 21st century demands that salespeople wake-up to some simple new realities. I often read books on sales and closing today that you need to have a doctorate degree to understand.

I like what Peter Daniels, the Australian millionaire, said and believe it is extremely appropriate for sales success in the 21st century: *"Selling is simple, you just tell the truth attractively."*

I am even often amazed at how complicated we make things as teachers and trainers. Life is complicated enough with all of the technology gadgets and so forth! Simplicity is a powerful thing in a world where things tend to be complex. You need to learn to K.I.S.S! (Keep It Simple Student)

This book is simply about Servant Selling! I believe that the time has come that in order to have lasting success we must gain the *trust* of our customers. When you operate as a Servant Seller, trust is the net result. When the customer sees, knows, and believes that you are there to serve them with your product or service, trust goes up.

Servant Selling

I was recently on site training in a large business where a Hispanic customer had made a very large installment purchase. After going home and showing the paperwork to family, someone implied that he had been ripped-off! I saw a young female Hispanic sales person struggling with explaining the payment agreement with the customer, so I went over and offered my assistance. I looked the customer in the eyes with all sincerity and explained the paperwork. He looked me in the eye and then turned and asked the young lady in Spanish. This guy seems sincere; can he really be trusted? She said absolutely! We shook hands, smiled and he left the establishment as a raving fan customer because I took care of another service issue related to the purchase. The young Hispanic sales person made a considerable commission on the sale because we employed the concept of Servant Selling.

The principles and concepts applied properly are sure to help you to find significance and success in sales as you serve your customers.

It's time to serve, sell, and succeed! Yes success and significance is yours through Servant Selling.

Servant Selling

SELLING IN THE 21st CENTURY

The 21st century is the information or knowledge age. In the information age in which we live, I can use my mouse and click my way into information such as the economic cycles of Singapore, or the demographics of Hong Kong. If you can click it you can have it, is the name of the game today. The power of the mouse has brought the hidden things to light. Sales people are wise to operate in "Servant Selling" in light of the new reality.

The long and short of it is that customers today have a serious information advantage and we in industry need to adjust our tactics and serve our customers. By the way, if you are a sales consultant I want to share with you some simple advice at the beginning of this book for the 21st Century that will make you big bucks in sales. *"Take care of your customer or someone else will!"* As the late great Henry Ford once said; *"If We Are Not Customer Driven, Nor Will Our Cars Be!"*

All great sales persons, managers and business owners understand that to have true and lasting success, they must be customer driven, particularly in such a highly competitive market. In Servant Selling, you will learn simple principles, practical skills and positive attitudes to help you sell more of your product and service your customers so that you achieve significance as a professional sales person and the financial success you deserve.

Chapter 2

The Vision

First, let's get a simple understanding of my *vision* for writing Servant Selling. A vision is a mental picture of a future state. My vision is to positively impact and change today's sales force to be Servant Sellers resulting in having sales people operate in positive principles of customer service that will help them sell more of their product or service, build lasting relationships with customers and prosper financially!

Many of the people influenced by this book will be the young or young at heart with an entrepreneurial vision. If this young sales force learns to operate in the right principles of Servant Selling, many will be millionaires by the age of thirty. I have seen these principles work in the automotive sale business, which is one of the toughest industries in the world. I have trained many sales people over the years, and the top 3% of them all operated by the Servant Selling concepts. Several of them ended up making more in some months selling that I did training. I could never figure that one out [the student making more than the teacher: that's the way of the world]. I would occasionally jokingly ask these Servant Sellers if they were hiring. *My vision is simply to change the world through Servant Selling.*

The Vision

GENERATION NEXT

I have a *vision* of a new generation of sales people rising up that will change the reputation that sales, particularly commission sales has gotten. Sales people are some of the least trusted people in our society. It doesn't have to be that way. Some people say – just keep dreaming boy. *I will.*
In Servant Selling I will give you some critical information about sales today. Selling is an honorable profession!

One major difference in selling in the 21st century is the workforce. As a corporate trainer, I have been pretty involved in the human resources area. It makes me feel a little bit old when I notice that most of our new sales people were not even born when I graduated high school. I often think are these kids just too young or am I getting old or what?

I really have a heart for the young. I like them! Many of the young today have entrepreneurial thinking. An entrepreneur is someone that takes a risk to make a gain. If they learn the power of **Servant Selling** and save and invest some of the money they make, I repeat that many will be millionaires at a young age! We have not majored on selling in our high schools or university systems. So, many of them go into corporate America to get a real job only to be down sized, right sized, left sized, or simply fired! I have never seen an organization down size sales consultants that were bringing in the bacon and helping the organization hear *Kaching* through Servant Selling.

The Vision

COMMISSION SELLING

Commission selling is definitely taking a risk, yet it is the greatest opportunity in business to make a great gain with little investment! Selling is a great place to learn critical business skills such as selling and negotiating.   Just check out Donald Trump and "The Apprentice." He is mainly teaching his young disciples how to sell and negotiate.

The contents of this book and the principle of Servant Selling properly implemented are guaranteed to increase the numbers and income of the average sales person and make them above average! I promise it WORKS!
The concepts are communicated in parabolic style, or a story. So let's go on a wonderful journey into Servant Selling so that you will experience sales significance and success that will get you out of debt and into abundance. By the way, even if you don't sell a product or service, I believe that you will find these principles to be universal, timeless, and important to everyday living.   You do sell the world's greatest product whether you are in professional, commissioned sales or not. You sell yourself! So keep reading.

By the way, I have written this book in parabolic, fictional style because I believe that stories communicate real life. The book features several characters that represent people in the marketplace today. Let your imagination soar and enjoy it. Joe Simple is waiting for us in chapter three. Remember K.I.S.S!

Chapter 3

Servant Selling Concept #1

"Stewardship"

Stew·ard *n.* One who manages another's property, finances, or other affairs

Joe Simple had finished the first phase of his training at EXCELLENT WAY AUTOMOTIVE GROUP. He had the weekend off and was about to get into *Servant Selling* sales training provided by EXCELLENT WAY. He had faded in and out of sleep all night due to his excitement about the start of the sales training program he would be entering the next morning. He thought throughout the night about the unlimited opportunity for both financial and professional growth.

Oscar Paywell, the owner of EXCELLENT WAY, had told him that the sky was the limit for him if he applied himself and stayed the course at EXCELLENT WAY.

Servant Selling Concept #1 **"Stewardship"**

Oscar had explained to Joe that he had several options. He shared with him that he was not just locked into selling for the rest of his career unless of course he chose to stay there, as many salespeople do. Oscar had told him his top three sales persons love selling so much that they never want to be managers. These top performers would offer support and mentoring for the new sales staff, but wanted to remain on the sales floor where the action is. However, Oscar assured Joe and explained his options. He knew that he could stay in sales, move into finance and/or operations management, work in the many support functions or become a dealer.

After being around Oscar and his positive influence during The Gospel of Customer Service class, Joe decided to do some research over the weekend on the auto industry so that he understood more of the psychology of the business he was getting into. While doing his online research he concluded that the automobile business was great because it was a nationwide industry and a sales pro can get a job <u>anywhere</u> in the nation in the profession of vehicle sales.

Servant Selling Concept #1 **"Stewardship"**

As Joe looked up at the ceiling fan twirling in the dark room with a tint of moonlight coming through the cathedral windowed ceiling, he contemplated about the automotive business being an entrepreneurial business with little or no financial investment required. He thought about his friend Jack Zipper who had invested most of his life's savings into a technology dot-com and lost it all on 9/11 after the terrorist attacks. He also recalled how he had lost what he thought was a "sure thing" chief technology officer position and lucrative income with Quality Plus, an Atlanta based technology firm. (Reader – please get a copy of my first book in the series Thank God It's Sunday! – The Gospel of Customer Service for that story a (www.iuniverse.com).

Servant Selling Concept #1 **"Stewardship"**

Joe thought to himself what a great deal, the Dealer provides:

- *A State of the Art Facility*
- *Training and Management Support*
- *Office Space, Phones, Computers*
- *Marketing and Advertising*
- *Finance, Parts, Service, Accounting, Clean -Up Dept*
- *Millions of $ in New/Used Inventory, and Equipment*

Joe pondered the fact that the dealer has the major investment yet, as a sales person, he would receive a significant share of the gross profit. He thought, not a bad deal. I think I am going to do some web surfing to check out the latest information on annual earnings in our area. Joe tipped toes in the dark out of the bedroom to go to his office and turn on his laptop to do a little more research.

Servant Selling Concept #1 **"Stewardship"**

Being a former information technology guru, he knew exactly where to go on the web for a comparison of earnings in his city. He went to www.salary.com and found:

Comparison of Earnings - Atlanta, GA.

Profession	Ave. Annual Earnings Range
Architect	$48 – 65K
Aerospace Engineer	$43 –51K
Software Engineer	$46 –58K
Accountant	$31 – 40K
Attorney	$64 – 83K

Servant Selling Concept #1 **"Stewardship"**

I OWE, I OWE! SO OFF TO WORK I GO!

Joe was thrilled when he recalled that Oscar had said the 12 of his Auto Sales Consultants at EXCELLENT WAY made over 100K in the previous year. Two of the twelve, had made over 200K! Joe then lay back in his large leather chair and thought to himself, "Thank God for this wonderful opportunity to provide the quality of life my family deserves." He looked at his clock and saw that it was only 4: 30am so he decided to go back to bed. As he lay there gazing at Jill, his beautiful wife with the moonlight shining in, he gave her a kiss on the cheek and said to himself, "Snooze –ville, here I come", and he drifted off into sleep.

As Joe was cruising down Interstate 85 in his BMW to go to the first day of sales training, he thought, "This is a wonderful occasion for a Starbuck's latte!" He pulled into the nearest Starbucks and jumped out of his car with a bounce in his step as he whistled his way though the front door. Starbucks was jumping with early morning espresso and caffeine fans.

Servant Selling Concept #1 **"Stewardship"**

Nancy, the manager, saw Joe come bouncing in and she said, "Hey Joe! How are you?" Joe said, "Nancy life is good! I'll take my favorite drink". Nancy said, "Coming right up Joe". Joe got his piping hot drink and left and the thought of giving ran through his mind so, he dropped a generous tip in the cash box on the counter and said thanks to Nancy. Joe looked at his watch and noticed that he was about an hour early so he decided to sit and read the local Atlanta paper while he enjoyed his coffee.

As he sat in a comfortable chair in the corner, he enjoyed the oldie hit music that was coming through the BOSE speakers, especially the SLY and THE FAMILY STONE hit "thank –u –fa - lettin – me – be –mice – elf – agin." Joe caught himself singing out loud, "I want to thank you…."

Nancy said, "Boy, you sure are in a good mood this morning Joe. What's up?" Joe said, "Nancy, I am on the top of the world looking down on creation." Nancy thought, "You're sure into your 70's jams also." Joe looked at her with glee and said, "After 9 months of unemployment due to the 9/11 crushing of our industry, I start a new job today". Nancy asked if it was in the hi-tech field. "No", Joe smiled. "It's at a car dealership". Nancy nearly choked on the cappuccino she was having as she forced a smile and said, "Good for you, Joe. I'm happy", as she walked back to the counter scratching her head. Joe just kept on humming, "I want to thank you for letting me be myself", as he sipped his java and looked through the business section of the Atlanta paper.

As Joe was looking through the paper, he noticed a large advertisement in the Barnes & Noble's section for Peter Block's classic book *Stewardship: Choosing Service Over Self Interest.* The title got his attention as he sipped on his sugar-free vanilla latte. The ad even defined the word steward to get the attention of the readers. It read: Steward defined; *one entrusted with, and responsible for, properly handling the goods of another.* Joe put the paper down and said to himself, "Stewardship. What a concept..."

Chapter 4

SALES – Your Path to Debt Freedom

Go, **sell** the oil and **pay** your debts!

Ancient Hebrew Precept

As Joe entered the training room at EXCELLENT WAY AUTOMOTIVE GROUP, he noticed a large motivational poster on the wall that said:

"Selling is one of the greatest skills of all time. The ability to persuade, Communicate and influence has been the basis of personal and financial success throughout the ages."
B. Tracy

As he was looking at the poster thinking of its meaning, he looked over and saw a young, handsome, well dressed black gentlemen sitting and reading a popular Zig Ziglar book entitled *Secrets of Closing the Sale.* Joe said with a bright smile, "Hi, I'm Joe Simple." The African-American gentlemen responded, "I'm Obbie Little. It's a pleasure meeting you Joe." Joe said, "I guess we are the first ones here." Obbie replied, "Mr. Paywell came through earlier with Sally Sellers to check out the room to make sure it was prepared for sales training. And, there is a young redhead lady named Jennifer here. She stepped out to the lady's room."

SALES – Your Path to Debt Freedom

As they looked around at the motivational posters on the wall, Obbie especially noticed one that said:

> **STEWARDSHIP**
> *Stewardship Is The Foundation of 21st Century Selling!*

As they were chatting about the positive motivational environment and discussing the Stewardship picture, Sally walked in and said hi to Joe and Obbie and told them that she would be their trainer for the Servant Selling training class.

Joe said, "But Sally, I thought you were in sales. I expected Oscar to do the training." Sally said, "Well Joe, I'm sorry to disappoint you!" Joe quickly said, "Oh no! I'm not disappointed at all!"

SALES – Your Path to Debt Freedom

"Oscar has decided to empower his top performers that have mastered the EXCELLENT WAY sales process by letting them teach the new recruits in the sales training class. I am the first on the schedule so you're stuck with me!" Joe said, "Oh Sally I think you are wonderful! I just assumed Oscar did all of the training." Sally said, "Joe, he did for years, but with the growth of the auto group he has decided to focus more on the overall strategic direction of the organization. However, he will continue teaching Thank God It's Sunday –The Gospel of Customer Service classes so that he stays close to the sales staff and keeps the spirit of customer service alive by imparting it to new people that join the team."

SALES – Your Path to Debt Freedom

"Oscar believes firmly that we are Stewards of the property, goods, and industry we are in. A steward always seeks to improve on the assets of another. He believes in us developing our full potential in every area. Oscar has a beautiful picture on the wall of his conference room that exemplifies stewardship. It's what Mr. Firestone said years ago:

> "It Is Only As We Develop Others
>
> That We Permanently Succeed."
>
> **Harvey S. Firestone**

Sally then said, "Yes, Oscar, being a steward of EXCELLENT WAY AUTOMOTIVE GROUP, certainly believes in the professional development of his people. For instance, he has asked me on several occasions to move into management and I have declined. I am having too much fun in sales taking care of my babies, my customers. I am a steward over my customer base. However, I am thrilled to have the opportunity to share concepts of sales excellence with this class. I consider that stewardship of my knowledge."

SALES – Your Path to Debt Freedom

As they stood talking, others began to stream into the training room, say good morning to Sally and head straight for the coffee, juice and goodies on the snack table. The table was loaded with pastries, fresh donuts, muffins, an array of cookies and even beef jerky for the Atkins Diet folks. After grabbing a snack while enjoying the music that set the atmosphere and mood for learning in the training room, the trainees started to sit and take a peek preview of the materials that were on the training table before them.

SALES – Your Path to Debt Freedom

When the twelve new students had taken their seats, Sally went to the front of the room and said with a cheerful voice, "Good morning! I'm Sally Sellers, your sales trainer for the week!" The trainees responded with a hearty good morning. Sally said, "So, I see we have a diverse group here." Approximately half of the group was either gen-x-ers or gen-y-ers.

Sally briefly told the group why she was doing the class. She then had them, one by one, introduce themselves and tell the rest of the group what their favorite hobby was. After the introductions she said, "When I took this job at EXCELLENT WAY, I was head over heels in debt. I have literally sold my way out of debt and into financial success. I am now a homeowner with three other pieces of investment real estate and a stock portfolio that is growing exponentially. You can sell you way out of debt and hear KACHING! because your income is up to you in commission sales." She then started to hand out the rest of the materials for the days training.

SALES – Your Path to Debt Freedom

Before she started the training class, she said, "By the way, we have a special trainee that is from the University of Alaska! He just graduated this May and has a desire to be an owner/dealer. His name is Obbie Little." Many in the class asked, "Wow, what's Alaska like?" Obbie said, "I will describe it this way. During the summer it's nice, but during the winter you are chilled to the bone!" Another young trainee said, "Man I bet you were chillin' like a villain!" The class laughed.

Big John, a middle-aged baby-boomer asked, "Why weren't you in the Gospel of Customer Service class, Obbie?" "Well, that's a long story…" Sally said to the rest of the group that had attended the Gospel of Customer Service class, "Obbie has been completing his college education in Alaska. I know we may seem to be putting the cart before the horse, but Oscar has signed off on him attending the sales class now and the customer service class later." Big John said, "Welcome aboard young buck!" Obbie just looked at him and smiled.

SALES – Your Path to Debt Freedom

PROFESSIONAL DEVELOPMENT

Sally walked over to the power point screen and pointed to the words:

> STEWARDSHIP
> *MEANS*
> PROFESSIONAL DEVELOPMENT!

She then said, "To start, I want to share some critical information, education, resources, and support materials you will need for success in automotive sales. If you want to succeed in sales and hear KACHING!, you must understand the K.I.S.S. Concept. One of the trainees spoke up and said, "Yeah, my last boss used to always say KISS – Keep It Simple Stupid!" As the class started to laugh Sally said, "That's okay however, we don't call our sales trainees stupid. We say K.I.S.S.: *Keep It Simple Student.* So, whenever I say K.I.S.S. during this class, you will know what I mean. Is that clear?" The whole class agreed.

K.I.S.S. *Keep It Simple Student!*

SALES – Your Path to Debt Freedom

"You must then go to work on the area of professional development. The key, though, is for you to take the attitude of a steward during this training class. I will entrust to you the best training and information I possibly can. But, it's up to you to value it and use it. Remember, the dealer is making quite an investment in you, so get into the mindset of being a steward. This philosophy is for people that want to excel. Take a look at this "commitment to stewardship" affirmation:

The Excellent Way Stewardship Affirmation

I am a steward of the more excellent way. I am responsible for, and entrusted with, the goods, vehicles, property and assets of the owner. I believe and understand that results are received only when hard work is put forth. I grow in the face of failure until excellence is obtained. I have a deep sense of loyalty and honor. I am committed to excellence. I firmly understand and believe that good is the enemy of best. I believe like the late, great Vince Lombardi that winning isn't everything; it's the only thing. I also agree with Aristotle that excellence is not an act, but a habit! I am committed to stewardship and sales excellence!

SALES – Your Path to Debt Freedom

GOAL SETTING

Sally then said, "Stewardship demands goal setting. Many see goal setting as just a motivational concept for the upwardly mobile success fanatic. But I have found goal setting to be solid, fundamental, pragmatism. So, to start out this training, let's spend some time talking about goal setting. Goal setting is crucial in the world of professional selling! Later in the training we will study the Rules of the Goals Game, which will further sharpen your goal-setting skills. To be successful in sales, you must understand: SMART goals."

Big John asked, "Smart goals? I don't understand. Are some goals dumb?" Sally said, "Pretty clever Big John. However, SMART is an acronym for the following. Look at the power-point screen please."

- **S - Specific & Measurable**: What will be accomplished?
- **M - Motivating**: Does the goal turn you on? Why?
- **A - Attainable**: Can the goal be accomplished?
- **R - Relevant**: How does this goal support your personal objectives?
- **T - Time-framed** When does this goal need to be completed

---

SALES – Your Path to Debt Freedom

"Specific means exact, to the point, focused. For example, if I asked you how much money do you plan on making in sales for the first year and you said "a lot", that would not be considered a SMART goal. Why? Just saying "a lot" of money is not specific. If you said "$79,000.00 in twelve months" I would say KACHING! Why? That goal is specific. Measurable simply means you are able to measure the progress of reaching your goal. Remember:"

K.I.S.S. *Keep It Simple Student!*

SALES – Your Path to Debt Freedom

Sally continued, "Why must a goal be measurable? Look at the following:

"IF YOU CAN'T MEASURE IT, YOU CAN'T MANAGE IT!"

Peter J. Daniels

Goals must also be attainable or achievable. To set a goal to make 1 million dollars the first year is probably not attainable for a new sales person. So, if you set a goal that is not attainable, you set yourself up for disillusionment!"

Setting and Managing Goals

The Most Successful Sales People Set Goals for:

- Family and Home
- Career and Finances
- Physical (Health)
- Spiritual and Ethics
- Social and Cultural
- Mental and Educational

SALES – Your Path to Debt Freedom

Sally then said, "I want you all to reach your goals. In fact, my job is to assist you in reaching your goals so that we at Excellent Way reach our goals. Remember to Use The Smart Goal Setting Program. Please take this program home and complete it by the end of training. One more important tip:

Goals Should Be Tracked <u>Daily!</u>

Now that we have the foundation, which is goal setting, laid let's talk some about being a professional salesperson.

Chapter 5

The Professional Sales Person

"The sales person is the most important

part of the sales transaction."

Zig Ziglar

Joe said, "Wait a minute Sally. I thought the customer was the most important part of the sales transaction. I have always been taught – **a "customer first" philosophy."** Sally said, "In that sense, the customer is first. I believe in the old saying *if you don't take care of your customer, someone else will*! But as far as the transaction is concerned, the sales person makes or breaks it." Sally then went to her power-point clicker to find the screen that said:

> "Seventy One Percent Of People Buy From You Because They Like You, Trust You, And Respect You."
> **New York Sales & Management Club**

The Professional Sales Person

▪   "If you can become this kind of sales person and not an old Car Dawg, people will like, trust, and respect you and your sales will go up significantly so that you continually hear KACHING!

By the way", Sally said, "People won't like you just because you are a nice person. Nice is relative. Remember *Al Capone's mother thought he was wonderful.* The moral of the story is that nice is relative to the people judging niceness. There are specific things that you can work on that will help you get an advantage as sales professional. **You must develop a vision of personal excellence."**

Don't be satisfied with being average! Average sales people never go to higher levels of sales income until they strive for excellence; to be the best in their industry.

> *"Good is the enemy of Best!"*

The Professional Sales Person

The professional does these things also, but goes beyond being average, or good, to being IRRESISTABLE. At EXCELLENT WAY we have defined twelve keys to being an irresistible sales person.

12 KEYS TO BEING AN IRRESISTABLE SALESPERSON

1. Professionalism – Be calm, confident, and reassuring
2. Dress for success – Clothes cover 95% of your body
3. Grooming – Your hair, nails, cologne
4. The brightness of your smile -:)
5. Your handshake – A firm, enthusiastic handshake
6. Eye contact – Make eye contact immediately
7. Lead the way – be a leader, not a dictator
8. Respect the customer – R.E.S.P.E.C.T!
9. Never prejudge – Communicate your sincerity
10. Be courteous and positive!
11. Learn to question skillfully
12. **Be authentic – *RELAX!* (or chill out!~)**

"Know yourself. You can't improve on something you don't know!"
Vince Lombardi

The Professional Sales Person

PERSONAL WORKSHOP

One way to get on the path of becoming an irresistible professional is to do this personal Workshop.

<u>Ask yourself honestly:</u>

Which of the 12 keys is your greatest strength?

_____

Which is your greatest challenge?

_____

What will you do to make up the deficiency?

_____

_____

_____

Remember: *"To Improve On Yourself Is Simply Common Sense.*
"Common Sense Is Not Always Common Practice"!
Take Action NOW!

The Professional Sales Person

2- 4- 6- 8 COMMUNICATE!

"The number one thing that makes a sales person <u>outstanding</u> to the customer is excellent communication skills."   **Bernard Smalls**

"The final concept I want to address in the beginning of our class is the development of communication skills. I call this section *How You Can Improve Your Communication Skills*. Successful sales people spend much more time listening than talking! First, you must understand and always remember what Zig Ziglar has said on so many occasions;

"When you're tellin', you ain't sellin!"

The Professional Sales Person

Here are 8 practical communication tips:

2. **When mentioning names, use full names.** If you say, "I saw Mary today", the listener may know several people with that name and this could cause confusion.

3. **Stick with the subject.** Very often people talk about one subject and, without warning, change to another subject. The result is complete misunderstanding of the issue. Watch out for "switches" in conversation.

4. **Avoid foolish jesting when dealing with customers.** People make remarks in jest or sarcasm, which very often are not recognized as such. The interpretation is often completely the opposite of what was intended.

5. **Always state your expectations clearly.** Two people may agree that something must be done, but each expects the other to do it. Always clearly state who is to do what and when.

The Professional Sales Person

6. **Preface your topic or subject.** People often start talking about a subject or problem without first providing the listener with the necessary background.

7. **When giving instructions, put them in writing.** If the instructions are complicated, "draw a picture" if possible, because "one picture is worth a thousand words".

8. **Share where you are in a transaction.** People need to see that progress is being made toward the goal that has been set. It's easy to become bored or panicky if progress is not seen. Boredom can cause a reduction in the productivity level. Panic can cause a person to go somewhere else for the product.

9. **People have a need to be kept informed.** Keeping the customer informed as things move along makes them feel like part of the team. Remember, everyone has their own perception of the deal-- not yours.

Perception Is Reality!

The Professional Sales Person

Finally, people need to have confidence in the person helping them; confidence based upon assurance of consistent fair treatment. Confidence will bring increased trust, loyalty and a feeling of security. Sally then said, "In developing your communication skills, you must understand **Perception VS. Reality."**

What people perceive that you are saying becomes their reality.

K.I.S.S. *Keep It Simple Student!*

The Professional Sales Person

LISTENING SKILLS

Developed listening skills will definitely help you in sales. You must make a conscious effort in this critical area. Think about what you say and how you say it. Put yourself in the role of listener. You may find out that what you think you are saying is not what is being heard. Listen completely like you care. Do not ever cut a person off mid-sentence. Pause and reflect on response; it makes them feel important. Here are three examples of good listening skills:

1. Focused attention; address all parties involved
2. Eye contact - jot down important points
3. Avoid interruptions during conversations

The Professional Sales Person

DRESS FOR SUCCESS

Sally then said, "Let's deal with the topic of personal appearance. We call it dressing for success: *Dress for Success* since it is one of Oscar's keys to being irresistible. You are also the steward of your body. So, how you dress is a reflection of your stewardship. I really like the saying, *"The body is a temple, don't treat it like it's a shed."* Some people have said to me while teaching this that they don't think clothing is that important because God looks at the heart. My reply is; He is the only one that does! People look at you: your clothes, your mannerisms, and your style! Remember that you never get a second chance to make a first impression. Your clothing covers approximately 95% of your body. The 21st Century sales consultant must understand the power of **Personal Appearance.**

> *"Clothes don't make the man but they sure do introduce him!"*

The Professional Sales Person

PERSONAL APPEARANCE

Because you are in a sales and service business, it is important to make a positive impression with your customers. Your goal is to have a conservative professional appearance while you are working. Business casual is the look of the day in most workplaces.

Hair – Well-groomed conservative haircuts are required. No ponytails, long hair, or odd colored hair. Beards and mustaches are to be kept short, and are not to be grown while working. If you do not wear a beard, you are to be cleanly shaved daily. Hats, bandannas, and other headwear are inappropriate for sales representatives.

Jewelry – In keeping with a conservative impression, a minimum of jewelry is best. Earrings are not acceptable for men. Multiple necklaces and bracelets should not be visible. A single strand necklace may be visible. No hanging medallions are to be visible.

Shirts – Wear the appropriate weight and style for the season. Short sleeves during warmer weather, long sleeves and sweaters during the cooler seasons. All shirts should be clean and well pressed.

Sweaters – Sweaters must be worn in the appropriate season: i.e. fall, winter, or in unusually cold spring weather.

The Professional Sales Person

Pants – Dress or Khaki material slacks should be worn if appropriate with your dealership. Slacks should always be well pressed.

Shoes – Black or brown dress or conservative casual or dress shoes with black or brown socks are required. NO SNEAKERS, BOATS, WHITE SHOES, OR TENNIS SHOES ARE TO BE WORN. Shoes should be kept shined and in good repair.

Suits – If a suit is appropriate for the selling environment, it should be conservative in color (black, dark blue, gray) and always well pressed and worn in the appropriate season. If a suit and tie are not required, I highly recommend an excellent business casual professional look. **NEVER, EVER LOOK SLOPPY!   Sloppy may be cool when you are hanging out, but it's expensive in the sales marketplace. Dress for success!**

The Professional Sales Person

RELATIONSHIP MANAGEMENT

Stewardship means relationship management in the sales process. This is so critical that I will address and re-address this topic throughout our training.

Relationship selling is the core of all modern selling strategies. Your ability to develop and maintain long-term customer relationships is the foundation for your success as a salesperson and your success in business. Relationship selling requires a clear understanding of the dynamics of the selling process as your customer experiences them.

For your customer, a buying decision usually means a decision to enter into a long-term relationship with you and your company. It is very much like a "business marriage." Before the customer decides to buy, he can take you or leave you. He doesn't need you or your company. He has a variety of options and choices open to him, including not buying anything at all. But when your customer makes a decision to buy from you and gives you money for the product or service you are selling, he becomes dependent on you. And since he has probably had bad buying experiences in the past, he is very uneasy and uncertain about getting into this kind of dependency relationship.

The Professional Sales Person

What if you let the customer down? What if your product does not work as you promised? What if you don't service it and support it as you promised? What if it breaks down and he can't get it replaced? What if the product or service is completely inappropriate for his needs? These are real dilemmas that go through the mind of every customer when it comes time to make the critical buying decisions.

The Professional Sales Person

Here are some keys to managing relationships with clients:

RELATIONSHIP MANAGEMENT IN SALES

1) Focus on the relationship – Not just the sale.

In many cases, the quality of your relationship with the customer is the competitive advantage that enables you to edge out others who may have similar products and services. The quality of the trust bond that exists between you and your customers can be so strong that no other competitor can get between you.

2) Maintain The Relationship – Never Take it For Granted

Once you have invested the time and made the efforts necessary to build a high-quality, trust-based relationship with your customer, you must maintain that relationship for the life of your business. You must never take it for granted.

The single biggest mistake that causes salespeople to lose customers is taking those customers for granted. It is when the salesperson relaxes his efforts in the relationship and begins to ignore the customer that failure will set in.

3) Engage in Consistent Action!

It Takes **Action Jackson! -:)** First, focus on building a high quality relationship with each customer by treating your customer so well that he comes back, buys again and refers you to his friends. Second, pay attention to your existing customers. Tell them you appreciate them.

The Professional Sales Person

Sally then walked out in the front of the training table, paused, and looked the group in the eye one by one and said, "Listen team. Stewardship is the critical element to your success both in this training class and once you hit the sales floor. Take ownership of what you are taught and when the class is over, treat the dealership like it is your own. You guys are wonderful and my commitment to you is to train you in such a way that you will be able to perform professionally and be the best you can be."

Chapter 6

Servant Selling *Concept #2*

SERVING

Servant: a person who serves others as **a:** an individual who performs duties about the person or home of a master or personal employer; **b:** a person in the employ and subject to the direction or control of an individual or company —see also <u>Source</u>: *Merriam-Webster Dictionary of Law, © 1996 Merriam-Webster, Inc.*

Sally told the class, "If you really want to succeed in sales and continually hear KACHING!, you must answer what I call The Big Question! which is – Who is the real boss?"

"Sam Walton, founder of Wal-Mart Stores, had it right when he said, *"The real boss is always the customer, and he can fire us at any time."*
Many look at this part of the class as a joke. But seeing yourself as a servant of the customer will take you to the top in sales. Someone would say, what does being a servant have to do with sales. Well, the root word for selling comes from a Scandinavian word that means to *serve*. A true sales professional is a servant of the customer. This brings us to what I call the Raving Fans Way. The best sales people today in every field have the heart of a servant which is the key to creating Raving Fans."

Servant Selling *Concept #2* **SERVING**

THE RAVING FANS WAY!

Sally had the whole group say out loud – THE RAVING FANS WAY!   Then she said, "This is what really put EXCELLENT WAY AUTOMOTIVE GROUP on the map and helped us win numerous customer service awards.   When Oscar was starting the dealership, he visited the Ken Blanchard Companies Training Campus in Escondido, California.   He was impressed there after reading Ken's book entitled *Raving Fans – A Revolutionary Approach to Customer Service*.   The Excellent Way would be the Raving Fans way.   Hooray for Ken and his excellent book.   The Raving Fans Way is revolutionary customer service for 21st century auto sales.

Let me explain.   As each new day, month and year of business arrives we will experience many changes.   Dealers must continue to anticipate change and respond by developing winning strategies to dominate the market.

It is imperative that we fully understand the rationale, procedures and strategies of "The Raving Fans Way."

We have found through our training process that Excellent Way/Raving Fans trained sales consultants are the best-trained people in the world of automotive sales and will be recognized throughout the industry as true professionals.

Servant Selling *Concept #2* **SERVING**

What is the "Raving Fans Way?" It is a simple yet effective approach to selling a vehicle for a salesperson and manager, as well as the best way to purchase a vehicle for our customers. This is because the sales person sees him or herself as a **servant** in the sales process. The customer becomes a raving fan and brags about the sales process and service they received. They (the customer) then become a part of your sales, marketing and advertising campaign.

This saves and makes the dealership money. Imagine each customer that buys from you as a walking, rolling advertisement for you. *It works!* The Raving Fans Way is based on three simple principles:

The Raving Fans Way

1. Decide what you want.
2. Discover what customers want.
3. Deliver plus 1%.

Decide – Discover – Deliver! I encourage you to visit your local bookstore today and obtain a copy of *Raving Fans – A Revolutionary Approach to Customer Service* by Dr. Ken Blanchard and Sheldon Bowles.

Servant Selling *Concept #2* **SERVING**

The Raving Fans Way is not just being nice or smiling. The process has been examined by some of the best business minds in the world and has been proved to produce extraordinary results. The Raving Fans process is non-threatening for everyone, yet allows the salesperson to re-position the consumer from non-buyer to buyer through a customer driven selection process that includes the following:

---

10 Key Elements of The Raving Fans Way

1. Professionalism

2. Excellent Treatment

3. Influence

4. Non-Confrontational Interview

5. Sharing of Vital Information

6. Integrity

7. Documentation

8. Flexibility

9. Management Support

10.   Customer Follow-Up

Servant Selling *Concept #2* **SERVING**

As each new day, month and year of business arrives, we will experience many changes. We are in the 21st century aren't we? Many dealers are still living by the rules of the 70's; the days of hot pants and platform shoes. You know, the pre-information age days. Back then you could tell customers just about anything, treat them rudely, and still survive. In the new model of selling, as Brian Tracy brilliantly calls it, the trust and relationship factor is critical to our success.

The New Model of Selling:	
The Trust Factor:	40%
Need Analysis:	30%
Presentation:	20%
Closing:	10%
The Sum: 100% Sales Success!	

The Raving Fans Way puts you 40% on the way to hearing KACHING! This is because it creates and fosters trust! Always remember that *71% of people buy from you because they like you, trust you, and respect you."* Let's examine The Raving Fans Process compared to the average sales person and their process.

Servant Selling *Concept #2* **SERVING**

The average sales person's process is based on self-serving greed and it is often done with the wrong attitude.

- ✓ Anything besides the attitude of service is the wrong attitude.
- ✓ Good processes with poor attitudes = a recipe for mediocrity!
- ✓ The Raving Fans Process is the basis for service excellence!
- ✓ The average, or old school, sales process is centered on the sales person.
- ✓ The Raving Fans process is centered on the CUSTOMER.
- ✓ The Raving Fans Process is not Average It's Extraordinary!

> *"The difference between ordinary and extraordinary is that little extra...!"*

Sally wrote on the board: **If you want extraordinary results, strive to be extraordinary.**

Servant Selling *Concept #2* **SERVING**

10 AFFIRMATIONS OF THE SERVANT/SELLER

The servant seller is a sales person that is a servant first and a sales person second. The reason sales have gotten such a bad rap is we have so many self-serving sales persons. Car Dawg managers that could care less about delivering raving fan service usually drive this attitude. These guys just generally have a negative view of life, not just sales, and it's tough to teach an old dawg new tricks! Oscar believes so strongly in these characteristics that he has trained every sales consultant to make these our daily affirmations. They are as follows:

1. I support my fellow associates and maintain a positive attitude at all times.
2. I conduct myself in a professional manner at all times.
3. I am open minded and enthusiastic about learning new information.
4. I serve at 100% at all times.
5. I don't engage in negative conversations that might adversely affect my own attitude or the attitudes of my associates.
6. I enthusiastically participate in all dealership activities believing that I will improve myself dramatically.

Servant Selling *Concept #2* **SERVING**

7. I work diligently to learn as much as I can and to become the best salesperson I can be.
8. I have fun at every appropriate moment.
9. When confused, I will recognize that I am learning and I will ask high-quality questions to clarify my confusion.
10. I always strive to be the best I can be – serving the Raving Fans Way!

Here is a quote that I hope will inspire you to an be extraordinary servant in sales:

> If a man is called to be a street sweeper, he should sweep streets even as Michelangelo painted or Beethoven composed music or Shakespeare wrote poetry. He should sweep streets so well that all of the hosts of heaven and earth will pause to say, "Here lived a great street sweeper who did his job well."
>
> Martin Luther King, Jr.

Servant Selling *Concept #2* **SERVING**

Why do you need to strive to be extraordinary in service today? Customers are very demanding today.

Sally asked the class to comment on how they thought customers saw car sales people today. The class was pretty unanimous in agreement that customers see car sales persons as car dawgs! In fact Joe even shared about a survey on CNN that talked about car sales people being the least trusted persons in the nation.

Sally thanked the trainees for their feedback and offered some facts based on a national survey of how customers see car sales people. "Remember, we don't want to get down on our industry, but the truth will set you free."

Servant Selling *Concept #2* **SERVING**

TEN CUSTOMER PERCEPTIONS OF A CAR DAWG

1. Pushy
2. Less Than Honest
3. Doesn't Listen
4. Uncaring
5. Focused On Our Own Agenda
6. Doesn't Follow Up
7. Non-Professional
8. Confrontational
9. Rude
10. Distrustful

Servant Selling *Concept #2* **SERVING**

At EXCELLENT WAY, we have found that there are three little questions every customer has in his/her mind when dealing with a car sales person. This is why we make the Raving Fans process a part of our best practices.   Every customer you meet will ask these three questions (mentally) about you and your dealership:

- Can I trust you, or are you just another car dawg?
- Are you truly committed to excellent service?
- Do you care about me as a person?

Obbie then said, "Sally, I don't mean to ask a dumb question but what's a car dawg?" Sally said, "Obbie, no question is a dumb question if you don't know the answer." Joe said, "Well, Sally, that depends. I've heard some questions that made me wonder if the person's wheel barrel was full of bricks or if their heads were!" The class all burst into laughter as Sally said, "Pretty good, Joe. Use that quick-wit on the sales floor and your customers will love you. Obbie, a car dawg is a slick, hustling, con-man, salesperson with dollar signs in his eyes. You need to understand that there are car dawgs and dawg catchers in this industry." Joe asked, "Now what in the world is a dawg catcher?" "Aha Mr. Quick wit! Now you have a question, huh?" Joe smiled and said, "Well...?" Sally said, "A dawg catcher is an educated consumer that is aware of the tactics of a car dawg."

Servant Selling *Concept #2* **SERVING**

"Since you have to effectively deal with dawg catchers, or intelligent buyers, that are out to catch car dawgs at their tricks, it's critical that we understand the characteristics of the sales professional. But first, let's take a ten minute break."

After the break Sally was standing in the front of the training room writing on the board. On the training tables were some chocolate goodies sitting in front of the training materials of each of the sales recruits. Big John said, "Wow! These are my favorites! You guys go all out!", as he chomped on a chewy chocolate turtle. Sally said, "Yes, you are my customers today. And, I believe in giving Raving Fan customer service."

Sally posed the question, "How many of you know that the word *sell* comes from a Scandinavian root word which means to *serve.* To me this means that a true salesman serves his customer!"

Servant Selling *Concept #2* **SERVING**

THE POWER OF VISION

Where there is no vision, the people perish...

Ancient Hebrew Proverb

Sally said to the class, "Let's talk about one of my favorite topics – Vision! Vision is the first secret to creating Raving Fans. So, let's gain a deeper understanding of the subject. Vision means you decide in advance what you want and envision what great service looks like. You must then deliver it to the customer, but that's another seminar. Let's just focus on vision for the moment.

You must have a positive vision in tough times.

Vision is not a result of success – success is a result of vision.

Your dream is your future! Vision is the result of dreams in action.

Nations with vision are powerfully enabled, without vision they perish. Family background and IQ can be overcome by vision. All that survived the concentration camp of NAZI Germany had something significant "yet to do" in their future. Victor Frankl, Man's Search for Meaning, said, "Vision is like a rope to get you across the turbulent waters of life." Money = the consequence of a vision achieved, vision is not the consequence of money.

Vision gives you the power to shape the future!

Servant Selling *Concept #2* **SERVING**

7 BEST PRACTICES OF VISIONARY SALES PEOPLE

Sally asked the class, "Have you ever thought about the fact that a visionary sales person is effective by using certain best practices? Vision and performance go hand in hand. Here are seven tips that will prepare you for being a Top Performer in the sales arena."

---

7 BEST PRACTICES

1. Read 30 minutes a day before starting the day, especially on selling.

2. Listen to something motivational all the time.

3. After every customer, interview yourself. Think and review.

4. Think Success not Failure!

5. Resolve to pay the full price to succeed.

6. Back your efforts with will power and determination!

7. Stay at it long enough to start winning - Persistence.

UNDERSTANDING THE VALUE OF PERSISTENCE!

The power to hold on in spite of everything, to endure – this is the winner's quality. Persistence is the ability to face defeat again and again without giving up – to push on in the face of great difficulty. Persistence means taking pains to overcome every obstacle, to do all that's necessary to reach our goals.

No, there is no failure for the man who realizes his power, who never knows when he is beaten; there is no failure for the determined endeavor; the unconquerable will. There is no failure for the man who gets up every time he falls, who rebounds like a rubber ball, who persists when everyone else gives up, who PUSHES TO THE FRONT when everyone else turns back!

O. Bernard Smalls

Servant Selling *Concept #2* **SERVING**

Sally said to the class, "As the immortal Winston Churchill said, NEVER, NEVER, QUIT! It's break time! Let's take ten!"

After the break, Sally walked back in while two of the sales trainees were commenting on how excellent the training was. She heard them but modestly smiled and walked over to the coffee machine to get some pep for the next session. She then walked to the front of the room and wrote on the board in bold letters: **Why People Buy!**

She then said, "Never forget that every person buys a car from you or from someone else! To be a top performer you need to understand that **every action in life is to better one's life.** Every prospect is dealing with the fear of loss and the desire for gain. Your job is to decrease the fear of loss and increase the desire for gain. The fear of loss leads to: let me think, I have to sleep on it, etc. This simply means that they don't have enough value reasons for buying.

No decision = I'M NOT CONVINCED!

Servant Selling *Concept #2* **SERVING**

When a person will not make a buying decision, it simply means that they are not convinced that the deal is in their best interest. Joe said, "Sally, this is all great stuff but how do you overcome this procrastination?" Sally said, "Glad you asked Mr. Simple. They key is determining the customers needs. This is profound, so don't miss it: **Need analysis is the beginning of all professional selling.** Need analysis means identifying the <u>key benefits</u> to the customer. Remember: **People don't buy products, they buy benefits!**

You could say people don't buy cars; they buy transportation solutions! Offer the right solution at the right price and you'll make the sale.

Servant Selling *Concept #2* **SERVING**

Let me introduce you to "The Six Honest Serving Men." That is just a fancy way of saying *six ways to ask questions to determine needs* or *why people will buy*. They are:

---

6 Honest Serving Men
1. **What** are you doing in this area right now?
2. **When** did you start doing this?
3. **Where** did you get your present product?
4. **How** did you start using this product?
5. **Why** are you thinking of changing?
6. **Who** else would be involved in the decision?

Sally said to her eager trainees, "It is critical in **Servant Selling** that you learn some basic psychology. How many of you have ever studied psychology?" About 40% of the hands in the class went up. Then Sally asked, "Have you ever hear of the concept of The Freudian slip?" Joe said, "Yes I have. It's a subconscious slip of the deepest concerns of a person." Sally said, "Well said, Joe. In selling, if you ask enough open and closed ended questions skillfully, you will eventually get some information that the customer was hiding. It just slips out, that's why it is called a Freudian Slip name after Sigmund Freud, the late, great founder of modern psychology.

Servant Selling *Concept #2* **SERVING**

The fact is most customers generally don't trust car salespeople. So, you must seek to uncover information in order to determine their need. Joe said, "Sounds like intelligence work." Sally said, "Right again, Joseph, but remember, it's intelligence work; not *interrogation!*

I was doing a class on professional selling at one dealership where the sales manager butted in saying, "What she is saying is good, but when you get the customer in, you must start your interrogation." That manager lasted about three months and was fired for poor performance. If you want to continually hear KACHING! Realize that people don't want to be interrogated! They are spending their hard earned money for a car!

Servant Selling *Concept #2* **SERVING**

UNDERSTANDING HUMAN NEED

The effective sales person is always interested in understanding their prospect. Here are some basic needs of every prospect:

1.   To be rich – security (just about everybody wants to be rich)
2.   To be liked -to be admired
3.   To be healthy
4.   To have prestige
5.   To be successful
6.   To have social status
7.   To have power
8.   To have influence
9.   To be up to date
10. To have comfort & security
11. To have companionship
12. To have potential realized
13. To not be missing out on anything
14. To have self preservation

Sally then enthusiastically said, "I think this screen says it all.";

> **Every customer's favorite radio station is:**
>
> **WIIFM?** *What's In It For Me?*

Chapter 7

RELATIONSHIP SELLING

Sally said to the class, "Let's revisit the topic of relationships in the sales transaction. All top sales people are relationship experts. Why? Customers need a friend, an adviser. Customers resist high pressure. You must understand that a key variable in selling in the 21st Century is RISK. Relationship Selling is effective because it lowers the risk factor. Relationship Selling is a skill that must be learned. Here are some key factors about relationship selling:

3 Key Facts About
Relationship Selling

1. **The relationship is hard to form because of the competitive culture.**

The decision to buy is a decision to enter a lasting relationship with our company.

2. **The more you focus on the relationship, the more the sale takes care of itself.**

Taking customers for granted is the main reason for lost sales.

3. **The relationship is valuable due to the low trust factor in today's markets.**

But, once formed, is easy to maintain if you pay attention to it.

RELATIONSHIP SELLING

"Since women are such major players in today's markets, let's take a brief look at Relationship Selling to Women. Research reveals that women are writing over 80% of all checks today. That's buying power, or should I say – GIRL POWER!!!" All of the female trainees began to cheer and whistle. Then Sally said in a dignified tone, "All right class, back to order please. Here is some simple information for relationship selling to women." Then Sally thought to herself and said, "I'll tell you what, guys. I'll include you, too. Is that fair?"

RELATIONSHIP SELLING

Let's take a look at my notes on "How to Sell to the Opposite Sex." Sally did a search on her IBM ThinkPad and found the power point presentation entitled: How to Sell to The Opposite Sex.

[GenderSell – Judith C. Tingley & Lee E. Robert How to Sell to the Opposite Sex]

The Gender-Sell approach is to use communication techniques typical of the other gender in order to increase potential for influence in sales situations.   Why understand Gender?   It's the Big Difference between Customers.   Or,   you   could   say,   Male   &   Female   differences   in Communication.

Men Influencing Women

- Women Want To Be Taken Seriously
- Give Female Customers What They Want
- Go Slowly
- Listen
- Ask More – Tell Less
- Talk About People And The Product Or Service
- Act In Accord
- Increase The Use Of Feeling Words And Emotional Events
- Avoid Giving Advice Unless Asked
- When The Sale Is Over, Keep In Touch
- Accept That Women May Be Higher Maintenance Than Men As Customers

RELATIONSHIP SELLING

Obbie started to laugh out loud and said, "You girls sure are high maintenance. But you are more than worth it." Sally said, "Thank you, Mr. Little, especially for the last line about us being worth it. It saved your neck!" Lets take a quick look at women influencing men in the buying process."

▪   **Women Influencing Men**

- Know Your Product – inside and out
- Take a Confident Tone
- Use Business, Money, and Sport Terminology
- Get to The Bottom Line – Be direct and specific
- Be Direct and Specific
- Make the Interaction a Win-Win Situation
- Use Humor & Lighten Up
- Decrease Emotional Intensity
- Calculate, Then Take Risks (guts impress.)
- **GET A MENTOR and Practice, Practice, Practice! (Find a male colleague and role-play)**

RELATIONSHIP SELLING

PERSONAL WORKSHOP

Write a paragraph on selling to the opposite sex. Then, share your thoughts in groups of three and then we will come together again.

MY THOUGHTS ON SELLING TO THE OPPOSITE SEX:

_____
_____
_____
_____
_____
_____
_____
_____
_____
_____
_____
_____
_____
_____
_____
_____
_____
_____

RELATIONSHIP SELLING

RELATIONSHIP NEGOTIATING

Sally said to the trainees, "Relationship negotiating is critical in selling in the 21st century. The old way of *"there is the price, take it or leave it"* will not work when people have information. Here are some key concepts in relationship negotiating. There are 3 Essential Parts:

> **1. To reach an agreement of some kind.**
>
> **2. To assure that all parties are satisfied.**
>
> **3. All parties are willing to negotiate again.**

In relationship negotiating, you want to build, not destroy, the relationship. You could look at it this way:

> **Relationships That Last = Win-Win or No Deal!**

Most car sales people know little or nothing about relationship negotiating. Most sales managers say *forget this relationship stuff, just go out there an start hammering*! Oscar often speaks of his early years when he was in sales. He talks about one sales manager that often said, "I only have one close: *"do you want to buy the blankety blank car or not?"* This kind of talk certainly doesn't build relationships with customers!

RELATIONSHIP SELLING

Relationship negotiating is far better than the fight for the wallet that happens in most dealerships. Most car dealerships have the unwritten motto: May The Slickest Guy Win! We Bait You! We Switch You! If You Don't Respond – WE DITCH YOU! Then they brag about being number one if the are the slickest; selling the most cars. I like what Lilly Tomlin said, "Even if you win the rat-race, YOU ARE STILL A RAT!" Who wants to be a rat? **That is not the case at EXCELLENT WAY.**

RELATIONSHIP SELLING

Here Are 4 Ways Customers Describe Relationship Negotiators:

1. He/She works for me.

2. He is a consultant, friend, and adviser.

3. He understands my situation.

4. I trust him/her.

The two simple keys to relationship selling are <u>Trust</u> and <u>Credibility</u>. The challenge we have in this business is that we are committed to Building Good Relationships in a negotiating culture. Some people say it can't be done. Oscar Paywell has proven that it can be done.

RELATIONSHIP SELLING

Now we will consider seven keys to building good relationships when selling a negotiable item:

1. Listening builds trust.

2. Lean forward and do not interrupt!

3. Pause 3 to 5 seconds before replying.

4. Consider what the customer has said.

5. Question for clarification; *well prepared questions.*

6. Feed it back.

7. Paraphrase in your own words.

Sally walked to the board and wrote: **"THE SOCRATIC METHOD"**
Joe said, "I'm familiar with that concept. It has to do with asking questions in selling." Sally said, "You got it, Joe. Remember; *When You Are Telling, You Are Not Selling.* When you are Asking Questions skillfully, you are selling professionally. Socrates, the great philosopher, was known for bringing people to a conclusion by asking questions versus telling them what they should do. How many of you like being told what to do?" No hands went up in the class.

RELATIONSHIP SELLING

Sally said to the trainees, "Here is a part of an article from "Classical Home-Schooling Magazine" entitled **What is the Socratic Method?** Written by Norris Archer Harrington.

John, a middle-aged baby-boomer who had lost his job as a Delta Airline pilot cried, "Home school? You'll use anything, huh, Sal!" Sally said, "If it makes the concept clear, in most cases I will. Thanks for the compliment John. Here we go."

Socrates, despite the contrary claims of his contemporaries, insisted many times that he was not an authority regarding anything. Almost without exception, he held that he was simply trying to understand the essence of whatever issue or question was at that time being discussed. When a seemingly wise man would make a bold proclamation regarding love, virtue, justice, or some other philosophical consideration, Socrates would respond by asking a simple question. When Meno, in the dialog that bears his name, asks Socrates, "Can virtue be taught?" Socrates asks, "Can you tell me what virtue is?" When Meno replies with a list of answers, Socrates notes that Meno has made something that was one into something that was many. Not very illustrative. He asks Meno if there is a single, unified definition of virtue. Thus begins a friendly dialog (not merely a technique) that discusses not only the essence of virtue in men, but also examines the very nature of knowledge and learning itself.

RELATIONSHIP SELLING

Thus, the Socratic Method is a conversation, a discussion, wherein two or more people assist one another in finding the answers to difficult questions. Why did Socrates proceed in this manner? Despite his many claims of ignorance, Socrates understood better than those with whom he spoke that it was not enough simply to "learn" facts, to memorize lessons, or to parrot lectures. To know truly, to seek wisdom, one must work toward understanding. If the question "what" leads us to see what we do and do not know, then the question "why" leads us to understand our world in a more full and fundamental manner.

> "Can virtue be taught?"
> - Meno
>
> "Can you tell me what virtue is?"
> - Socrates

RELATIONSHIP SELLING

"Yes" questions are the key in **Servant Selling**.

Here are some powerful Relationship Negotiating Questions:

- *What do you have in mind?*
- *What else?*
- *Do I know everything I should know?*
- *Is there another possibility?*
- *What would it take to…?*
- *Is the offer clear?*
- *What if, or suppose that…?*
- *Now that you have told me what you want, what do you need?*
- *What's your offer?*
- *Could you repeat that offer?*

RELATIONSHIP SELLING

RELATIONSHIP CLOSING

Let's take a quick look at Relationship Closing! First, you must understand that closing is the most stressful part of the sales <u>relationship</u> for the sales person and the customer. Remember what I said earlier:

1) The fear of failure is 80% of the reason the person refuses to make a buying decision.

2) The fear of rejection is 80% of the reason that the sales person refuses to ask for the business.

Here are 4 Conditions that must be met in relationship closing:

1. The Customer needs it.

2. The Customer can use it.

3. The Customer can afford it.

4. The Customer wants it.

Here are 2 confirming questions before attempting to close:

1. Do you have any questions or concerns I haven't covered?

2. Does this make sense to you so far?

RELATIONSHIP SELLING

The sum of relationship, which is the core of **Servant Selling** is: **"VALUE TO THE CUSTOMER".**

Sally then asked the class to answer the discussion questions before they took a break for lunch. She said, "It's just about lunchtime and, by the way, Joe is buying!" Joe said, "No way, Jose! Not yet. Let me get a few sales under my belt first and get a *fat check*."

RELATIONSHIP SELLING

After lunch, Sally said, "Let's wrap up our training on the psychology of selling. In every sale there are two major factors in the prospects mind:

1. **The key benefit**
2. **The key issue** (price, competition)

Some other factors are the 80/20 rule, or the Pareto Principle, which means **80 percent of the decision is often in 20 percent of the benefits.** Ask closing questions: i.e. "If you were ever to buy our product, why would you?" Once the customer has told you why they would buy the vehicle, you now have their hot button. Now, use the hot button close! How? By continually talking about their hot button, or reason for buying. Remember WIIFM? The hot button is the customer's WIIFM! In psychology it is said that it is impossible for an intelligent person to make a conscious decision that will make their lives worse. People generally make buying decisions when they think that they will be better off, not worse. Do you agree?

K.I.S.S. *Keep It Simple Student!*

Chapter 8

REACHING YOUR
PROFESSIONAL SALES POTENTIAL

Sally said, "Let's take a look at one of my favorite topics: Reaching your Full Potential in Sales. Here is a sheet that was not in your training manual." Sally hands the sheet to the persons sitting on the end of each table and asks them to pass the sheet around. The outline read:

"THE POTENTIAL POWER OF KNOWLEDGE"

Here are 3 areas of knowledge you must have to be a SERVANT/SELLER:

1. **Know Your Customers & Their Needs**
   Search for Closing Information

2. **Know Your Products and Services**
   We Must <u>Add Value</u> to the Process to Maximize Profits

3. **Know Your Market**
   Always Know More Than the Most Informed Customer
   Work Your Prospecting Strategy <u>Everyday</u>

REACHING YOUR PROFESSIONAL SALES POTENTIAL

KNOW YOURSELF

Let's analyze the concepts of developing your full potential in sales one by one. There are three major concepts. The first concept is to know yourself.

1)   KNOWING YOURSELF!

"Above all other admonitions, know thyself!" Shakespeare

Here are five things you should know about yourself as it relates to servant selling:

1. Your Attitude Is EVERYTHING!
2. The Customer Knows and Feels Your Attitude Instantly
3. Your Attitude Controls Your Enthusiasm & Energy
4. Your Enthusiasm & Energy Controls the Sale
5. Accept That You Choose Your Attitude

"Life is 10% What Happens to You, 90% How You Respond to it!"

Charles Swindoll

I love the topic of attitude. I have found that Attitude Prep Requires Daily Focus! And never forget:

Attitude Controls Altitude!

REACHING YOUR PROFESSIONAL SALES POTENTIAL

KNOW YOURSELF

Sally said, "If you will turn to the back of the training room and look at the back wall, you will notice that we have Ten Secrets Of Success. They display the attitude of the winner in sales and in life. If you make these a part of your thinking, your self-awareness will certainly increase because they are like a measuring stick to constantly compare yourself to. The class turned around to look at the large white board that read:

THE TEN SECRETS OF SUCCESS

1. How you Think is Everything!

2. Decide Upon your Dreams and Goals

3. Take Action

4. Never Stop Learning

5. Be Persistent – Work Hard

6. Learn to Analyze Details

7. Focus Your Time And Money

8. Don't be Afraid to Innovate

9. Deal and Communicate with People Effectively

10. Be honest, Dependable and Responsible or 1-9 won't matter!

REACHING YOUR PROFESSIONAL SALES POTENTIAL

Joe said, "This is great, Sally. I especially like number 10. That's the clincher." Sally replied, "Thanks for the feedback Joe. Yes, number 10 is where the rubber meets the road, and that's usually the toughest one for sales people to keep. It takes hard work and commitment. Remember: know yourself!"

REACHING YOUR PROFESSIONAL SALES POTENTIAL

KNOW YOUR CUSTOMERS

Let's take a look at the next critical area of developing your full potential in servant/selling in the 21st century. It is:

2)   KNOW YOUR CUSTOMERS!

UNDERSTANDING THE PSYCHOLOGY OF CUSTOMERS

Some call it behavioral selling. It relates to understanding the prospect and his/her motivation. To be successful in sales you don't need to have a degree in the behavioral sciences of psychology. However, there is much psychology involved in selling and buying. A basic understanding of human personality is critical in the world of professional selling. We call it DISC. Several years ago Oscar attended a Carlson Learning Center DiSC seminar and he has done extensive teaching and training to all of his managers on the concept. I will give you and overview.   DiSC is about understanding personality types. Oscar had you complete the AVA personality test to determine your personality type. If you were high on assertiveness and sociability you have a great sales personality. If you were high on conformity and calmness, you are not a bad sales person but you might not fit into a competitive sales culture. Great sales people are "confident people persons", for lack of a better phrase.

REACHING YOUR PROFESSIONAL SALES POTENTIAL

The DiSC Profile is a tool to help us understand others and ourselves. The DiSC Profile was designed by the Carlson Learning Center of Minneapolis, Minnesota and is successfully used by all types of businesses and organizations. DiSC is a basic but powerful psychology tool that helps you understand yourself, helps read the customer, helps you be the best and helps you make a quick transition from b.s. (behavioral sciences) to c.s. (common sense).

THE DISC PROFILE GOALS

- GOAL ONE: Understand your work behavioral tendencies and how they affect others.

- GOAL TWO: Understand, respect, appreciate, and value individual differences.

- GOAL THREE: To enhance your effectiveness in accomplishing tasks by improving your relationships with others.

- GOAL FOUR: To develop strategies for working together to increase productivity and sales by understanding our customers.

REACHING YOUR PROFESSIONAL SALES POTENTIAL

Understanding DiSC: The Four Temperaments

Here is a quick outline of the four personality types. You will meet these four types of customers over and over in sales.

D: Dominant – Aggressive and Demanding!

I: Influencing – People Oriented and Interactive

S: Steady – Cautious and Calculating

C: Compliant – Conforming & Easy going!

The real power behind the disc concept is you know your customer and his/her needs. In essence, <u>disc is a tool</u> we can use to read customers.

"The Power to Adjust to the Prospect's Temperament is the Key to Building Rapport!"

Bernard Smalls

REACHING YOUR PROFESSIONAL SALES POTENTIAL

"Learning" our prospect is critical in professional selling. This often starts with the sales interview or need analysis, which we will cover later. Here are some key insights you must have to be successful with today's customer:

Customers Must Perceive Your Value ASAP!
1. Customer Comfort/Your Value = KACHING!
2. Control the "Process"-- <u>Not</u> the Customer!
3. Customer Control = "Up Goes the Walls!"
4. Let the Customer Feel in Control.

REACHING YOUR PROFESSIONAL SALES POTENTIAL

After you have done "the DiSC thing" you are better positioned for identifying customer needs. Seek closing points from the customer probes: "tell me more"; "why do you say that"; "what else should I know"? The major reason for using disc is so that you can build rapport and get information or closing points if you would: listen closely and write down the information, show the customer you're listening (the nod), listening adds value, adding value adds gross profit!   Sally concluded this section by saying, "We will talk more in depth about the four personality types when we look at the fundamentals of selling."

REACHING YOUR PROFESSIONAL SALES POTENTIAL

KNOW YOUR PRODUCT

3)   KNOW YOUR PRODUCTS/SERVICES

Now that you have gotten to know your customer, you must display that you know your products/services. Always share "why buy here" info which is the organization's "added value."   Every business has certain competitive advantages, meaning, you only get this when you buy here.
You should review new and used stock daily. It is important that you know what you have to sell! It is important to know what <u>is</u> and <u>is not</u> available!

Product expertise is not an option. According to a national survey, 80% of customers don't think the salesperson is knowledgeable. Product knowledge is a major element of "adding value." Remember the car is that 2nd largest investment for the average customer.   If you don't know the product, you could have a credibility issue. We're selling high ticket/high tech products, not bubble gum (no pun intended if you are a gum salesperson!) Product knowledge also generates belief in your product. *You can't believe beyond actual knowledge.*   **Belief in Your Product is Contagious!**

REACHING YOUR PROFESSIONAL SALES POTENTIAL

It is also important to know your market or your floor traffic. Customer education varies dramatically. Don't assume any level of information. ***Know who you're dealing with!*** How do you get customer education?   Ask the customer if they've researched vehicle and trade information.   If yes, what sources?   If the Internet, ask which websites? What information led to vehicle selection?

The "informed buyer" is the 21st century challenge! I have found that it is good to know where the customer finds info.   Here are just a few sources of information for automobile sales professionals:

- o Edmund's. com
- o Autotrader.com
- o Intellichoice.com
- o KBB.com
- o Autobytel.com
- o Your Manufacturers website
- o Consumer Reports
- o J.D. Powers & Associates

We Must Be More Informed Than the Most Informed Customer!

REACHING YOUR PROFESSIONAL SALES POTENTIAL

I guess the real question is *"Who's the Pro?"* Oscar taught me this phrase when I first started and it's made me a motivational information guru:

Knowledge = Potential Power!

Sally added, "The first type of customer you should know and understand is the invoice shopper. The invoice I am talking about is the dealer invoice or basically the wholesale price of the car, or what the dealer paid for the car. Since this information is available on the Internet, you had better know how to do business with the invoice shopper."

The "Invoice Shopper"

When a customer wants to buy your vehicle at invoice here are some selling tips:

1) Never argue with the customer.

2) All the same negotiation rules still apply.

3) Ask kindly: is the dealer entitled to a profit?

4) Ask the customer: is dealer invoice really dealer "cost"?

If they say yes ask what about:

- *Floor Plan Costs*
- *Facility Investment & Overhead*
- *City, County, State, Payroll, S.S., Federal Taxes*
- *Insurance*
- *Personnel Costs*

REACHING YOUR PROFESSIONAL SALES POTENTIAL

What do you think is "Fair" considering your understanding of invoice plus…?

Sally walked over to the board and wrote:

True or False:

Invoice Buyer = Lower Average Gross

Is this true or false? About 80% of the training class said that was true. Joe said, "I don't think it's true or false." Sally said, "Hah! Why do you say that Joe?" Joe said, "I'm not exactly sure that invoice customers always mean less profit." Sally said, "You are touching on something Joe. My answer to the question is that it is not true or false. Here is the key concept:

IT DEPENDS!

REACHING YOUR PROFESSIONAL SALES POTENTIAL

Always remember that in selling, the principles are not a hard science like math: i.e. 2+2=4 all the time. But, in selling, it depends on the situation, the customer's personality, how much they want and need the product. Never forget – **IT DEPENDS!**

The key to making a profit when dealing with the invoice buyer is to develop your negotiating skills. Let's take a close-up of this topic. Look at the screen, Sally clicks her mouse and the words appeared in bright red:

Developing Negotiation Skills

"Never fear to negotiate, and never negotiate out of fear!"

John F. Kennedy

Excellent Negotiating Skills will help you to sell more of any product or service! You should always work to improve your skills in this critical area. Always mentally evaluate after a deal. Always be a student of the art and science. Always understand that negotiating is an art and science!

REACHING YOUR PROFESSIONAL SALES POTENTIAL

Sally said, "Many people when buying a car will say, *I don't want any of the back and forth stuff. Just give me your best price.* But, I have found that negotiation skills are not an option in any business. We negotiate for furniture, jewelry, real estate, supplies, services, personnel, equipment, you name it! Is America not a negotiation culture? Oscar teaches what he calls win-win negotiating. He says that's the only way to build a relationship that will last with the customer.

Here are some key benefits of Win-Win negotiating:

---

3 Benefits of Excellent Negotiating Skills

1) Repeat Business

2) Referrals

3) High Customer Satisfaction Index (CSI)

REACHING YOUR PROFESSIONAL SALES POTENTIAL

Obbie said, "This is some of the best training I have ever had in any setting. In some ways it reminds me of when I was in college, pursuing my education.   I think I'll start calling you professor Sellers!"   Sally simply smiled at Obbie's comment and said, "Oscar is a firm believer in continuous education through training. He believes it's the key to fluency.   So we encourage you to respect the owner's investment in you."

REACHING YOUR PROFESSIONAL SALES POTENTIAL

Obbie raised his hand and asked, "Sally, in what context do you use the word fluency?" "Great question Obbie. To me, fluency is the combination of accuracy plus speed of performance that characterizes competence or true mastery! It simply means you have become the best at what you do. To illustrate this, I was watching E-TV last night as they showed the upward trajectory of the Williams sisters in tennis. When they started out, they had athletic ability but were not very fluent in the game of tennis. Through practice and much training (especially from dad), they both became fluent, or the best at the game. Anyone great is fluent at what they do whether it is public speaking, music, art, sports, and, yes, selling! How do you get there? Well, we believe that excellent training is the foundation stone. You must build upon the solid ROCK of great, effective, training."

Sally then walked over to the music system and hit the button. As Sly and the Family Stone's "Want to Take You Higher" piped out she said, "It's break time guys."

REACHING YOUR PROFESSIONAL SALES POTENTIAL

After the break, the group found huge macadamia nut cookies with a blue and gold ribbon around the plastic packages with a note from Oscar that said, "I believe in you!" The class was blown away by the owner's caring heart and attention to detail. Big John said, "Get Down Baby" as he tore open his package and started to munch. Several in the class wanted Mr. Paywell's email address so that they could express their thanks. Sally gave it to them and said enjoy the cookies.

Let's look into the major concepts I want you to grasp through this training program as we prepare to move into sales process.   Look at the screen please:

Major Concepts!
Understanding The Psychology of Sales
Understanding The Fundamentals of Sales
Understanding How to Make A Profit While Serving Your Customer

REACHING YOUR PROFESSIONAL SALES POTENTIAL

Sally said to the class, "Now repeat after me KACHING!" They all did! Finally, remember that in the 21st century sales, customer satisfaction is not good enough! You must exceed their expectations and create Raving Fans if you want to continually hear KACHING! You must serve as you sell! Yes, Servant Selling is the real key to financial profitability.

Chapter 9

Servant Selling Concept #3

Selling

"Understanding the Psychology of Selling"

Sell what you have.... *Jesus*

Sell – defined;

- To exchange or deliver for money or its equivalent.
- To offer for sale, as for one's business or livelihood: *The partners sell textiles.*
- To give up or surrender in exchange for a price or reward: *sell one's soul to the devil.*
- To persuade (another) to recognize the worth or desirability of something: *They sold me on the idea.*

Lets get into the meat of our training while we talk about one of my favorite topics: the concept of selling. Joe Simple said, "With a last name like yours Sally, that figures." Sally said, "I think we should change your last name to Joe Smart", as the class roared.

Servant Selling Concept #3 **Selling**

Sally went on to say, "Oscar, our owner, calls this servant/selling, the integrity based sales process. In fact, Oscar has put this on a card that will help you to remember. As she passed the cards around, the trainees noticed that it read:

Two Cardinal Rules to Servant/Selling:
Rule #1) Create Value For Customer. Rule#2) There will be no Other Rules!
                    The Sum: Value To The Customer!

Servant Selling Concept #3 **Selling**

UNDERSTANDING THE PSYCHOLOGY OF SELLING

Sally told the group, "Now its time to stretch a little. This is called "Reach for the Roof!" Put your right hand up first, then your left hand, now stretch as far as you can as if you were literally reaching for the roof. Doesn't that feel good? Now let's stretch our minds and take a close look at the concept of selling. First, we must understand that in life we are always selling or being sold. Life is like a game or process of selling.

SELLING IS SIMPLY THE POWER OF PERSUASION

You sell your kids to be good.

You sell your spouse that you are a good mate.

You sell your significant other that you are the one!

Politicians sell their political agenda.

Preachers and religious leaders sell people on their faith.

We live in a world of sales.

Servant Selling Concept #3 **Selling**

Now that you have chosen selling as your profession, it is critical that you understand how to play the game and win. Let's talk about "The Inner Game of Selling." We will look at the characteristics that separate top performers from the herd in sales. When I use the word herd, it's not a put down. It simply refers to the 80% of sales people that follow the follower. They tend to remain mediocre in sales. There is a motivational principle called the 80/20 rule, or the Pareto Principle. Mr. Pareto was an Italian economist that found that in most numerical situations, the 80/20 Rule applied. For example, 80% of the sales on a sales floor are normally made by 20% of the sales people, and 20% of the sales are normally made by the remaining 80% of the sales people. Based on this principle, which would be the herd, the 80 are the top 20% of the sales people. Joe said, "The 80% would be the herd." Sally said, "Excellent Joe, you're exactly right.

Servant Selling Concept #3 **Selling**

One of the major keys to sales success is to get into the top 20% of the sales staff. The people in the top 20% understand that their job is simply persuading the prospect that their product meets the prospects need and getting the order. K.I.S.S!

K.I.S.S. Keep It Simple Students!

Servant Selling Concept #3 **Selling**

To truly be effective as a servant/seller, you must *think* and be different.   In other words, your thoughts control your life. Your thoughts control your sales success. I am going to share in this session some suggestions or concepts on how you can renew your mind or thoughts so that you can be effective. First, you must understand that sales effective is life effectiveness. I like what Mr. Ziglar says:

> *"It's Not the Sales Person That Sells,*
> *It's The Whole Person That Sells!"*
>   **Zig Ziglar**

Servant Selling Concept #3 **Selling**

Les Brown, the motivator, says; *people buy you before they buy your product.* Here are some things that top performers understand according to Brian Tracy, the author of The Psychology of Selling. **There are two things you must get clear on:**

1. **Understand that selling is an honorable vocation.** In other words, you must feel good about being a professional sales consultant to be a top performer. There is an old saying in the world of sales that you must make note of. It is; "Nothing Happens Until In Our Economy Until Somebody Sells Something!"

2. **You must understand the power of the self-concept.** This affects every area of life. You never act in a manner inconsistent with your self-concept. You never earn more outwardly than you do inwardly. Deal with the mental blocks; *see yourself* as the best in your mind. The late Dr. Maxwell Maltz was known for saying;

"The Me I see, Is the Me I'll Be!

Servant Selling Concept #3 **Selling**

Sally said to the class, "To stay ahead of the pack, you must master the **six areas of selling**. I want to give you a preview of this topic, which we will dissect later in the training. No matter what you sell, these six factors will be a part of the sales process. Believe me, I have done it month after month for the last twenty-four months at EXCELLENT WAY. Take a look at the screen:

THE SIX FUNDAMENTALS OF SELLING

1. NEED ANALYSIS
2. PRESENTING
3. CLOSING
4. GETTING REFERRALS
5. FOLLOW-UP
6. PROSPECTING

Self-limiting beliefs are one of the main reasons for failure in sales. These beliefs are often built on erroneous material or simply said, "wrong thinking or stinking thinking". Renew your mind! Your thinking affects your self-concept, and your self-concept controls your performance. A daily check up from the neck up is critical if you are going to be a leader in sales! The reason is;

"You Become What You Think About!"

Earl Nightengale

Servant Selling Concept #3 **Selling**

Sally then looked at her beautiful Rolex watch that she had won for being salesperson of the year and said, "Oh my goodness. It's already 10:15! It's past your break time. Take an extra 5 minutes on me... See you in 15 minutes instead of the usual 10."

Servant Selling Concept #3 **Selling**

TWO BIG FEARS!

> *"Do the thing you fear and the death of fear is certain."*

Anonymous

After the break, Sally welcomed the class back and said, "Let's discuss the fear factor in sales. The amazing thing that I have learned in success motivation concepts is FEAR IS THE GREATEST REASON FOR FAILURE! There are two big fears involved in the sales process. The "Big Two", as I like to call them, can be conquered by developing your self-concept. The power to excel in sales is released as you overcome these. The more you like yourself the easier it is to overcome these. The "Big Two" are the fear of failure and the fear of rejection.

First, let's deal with the fear of failure. This fear is simply the fear of making a mistake. This fear is usually on the part of *the customer*. They fear making a mistake in buying your car and going home seeing an ad in the paper for the same car at a much better price. This holds more buying decisions back than anything else. This fear is sometimes in the sales person and the customer. The sales person fears losing or not making the sale, which to them is considered failure.

The second is the fear of rejection. You must prepare to handle rejection. This fear is usually predominant in *the sales person*. This is the fear that the customer might say NO!

Servant Selling Concept #3 **Selling**

"80% Of Sales Are Made After The 5ᵗʰ Closing Attempt, Yet Only 10% Of Sales People Make More Than Five Attempts To Close!

DEALING WITH REJECTION

Now think about this. Since approximately 80% of initial sales calls end up in a NO, if you can't handle rejection, you have chosen an interesting way to make a living. **YOU WILL BE REJECTED!** Rejection is a part of selling, get use to it.

With no fear of rejection you would be a top performer in sales. I consider this to be profound. Since this is true, you should not fear rejection and keep on politely asking for the business. All greats have overcome the fear of rejection.

Here is another statistic to understand to help you sell more cars:

"80% Of Sales Are Closed After The 5ᵗʰ Attempt, Yet 48 % Of All Sales Ends With The Sales Person Only Attempting To Close Once."

What's the reason they only ask once? They Fear Rejection! Joe raised his hand and asked Sally, "How do you overcome these two big fears?" Sally said, "Good question Mr. Simple. It's very simple – you learn how to cash in on self-concept." Sally said, "I want you to read the section again within the next twenty-four hours and think deeply on how powerful it is."

112

Servant Selling Concept #3 **Selling**

CASH IN ON A POSITIVE SELF CONCEPT

Sally walked to the large flip chart and flipped to the colorful sheet that said:

"Selling is a Transference of Feeling!"

Often, this feeling starts with how you feel about yourself. The area of self-concept is one of the most critical areas of selling. It is so critical, I will talk about it again later in the class. Have you ever noticed that when you feel bad about yourself, it's hard to persuade others? So, here are five things you can do to cash in on self-concept and develop a positive self-concept, check out the screen:

Cashing In On Self Concept In Sales!

1. Make a decision to build your own self-esteem!

2. Rejection is not personal.

3. Be diligent – work hard & smart.

4. Positive self-talk. (Saying "I can" instead of saying "I cannot")

5. Motivational books, tapes & training.

Servant Selling Concept #3 **Selling**

PSYCHO SALES PERSON

Now, here is some of the most critical stuff you will ever learn in selling yourself so that you can more cars. You must Develop A Powerful Sales Personality.   Remember the great Joe Girard, the world greatest salesman said: "I don't sell cars, I sell myself!" In order to do this you must understand the professional sales personality.   Here is a psychological profile of the successful servant sales professional.

The Psychological Make-Up Of A Successful Servant Seller	
1.	High Self Concept
2.	100% Responsibility For Results
3.	Above Average Ambition & Desire (Extra Effort)
4.	High Levels Of Empathy (Cares About The Prospect)
5.	Intensely Goal Oriented (Weekly, Monthly, Yearly)
6.	Above Average Will Power And Determination To Succeed
7.	Belief In Self, Product, And Company (Sell The Right Product)
8.	Easy Ability To Turn Strangers Into Friends.

Servant Selling Concept #3 **Selling**

Sally asked the class, "What do you think are the two main characteristics of top sales performers?"   A young, clean cut Hispanic trainee named Jose said, "I think it's passion and product knowledge."   Sally said, "Good try, Jose but that's not quite what I'm looking for. Anyone else want to take a stab at it?", asked Sally.   Joe said, "I think one of the qualities would have to be goal setting."   Sally asked, "Joe, why do you say that?"   "Because, in all of my personal development training, goal setting has been high on the list."   Sally said, "You are right, Joe. Goal setting is one of the characteristics. What's the other?"   Joe said, "I really don't know specifically."

Servant Selling Concept #3 **Selling**

Obbie said, "This may seem a little strange but I believe it is vision, or seeing the end when you begin." Sally said, "Hmmm, and why do you say that, Obbie?" "Because, I am presently reading *7 Habits of Highly Effective People* and Dr. Covey puts a lot of emphasis on that concept." Sally said, "Obbie, you are right! All top performers visualize the result they want before they start. Even people like Tiger Woods use visualization. You've seen the TV commercial about him putting where he saw the different angles of the potential stroke haven't you?" About 50% of the class said yes. Sally then said, "Be a tiger. Set the goal and visualize success. So the two psychological characteristics of all top sales performers are:

1) Goal Orientation and 2) Visualization.

Servant Selling Concept #3 **Selling**

Let's take a look at how Goal Orientation and Visualization apply to sales success. Look at the screen please:

GOAL ORIENTATION

When You Set A Goal You Program Your Subconscious Mind And Start It To Take Rapid Action Towards Your Goal. You Recognize More Opportunities.

Sally said, "Set personal and family goals, and goals of things that you want to accomplish. Develop many reasons for achieving your goal; a new home, a new or great pre-owned car, trips, jewelry or whatever you have dreamed of having. Then you should set performance and productivity goals. Carefully plan your working day, week, and month. And of course you must set income goals. How much do you want to earn this year?"

- Monthly goal
- Weekly goal
- Daily goal

Servant Selling Concept #3 **Selling**

"The second characteristic of all top performers is visualization. When you say visualization today, many think of eastern religion. But, I am talking about seeing the end result that you want. Visualization is actually a critical part of accomplishing your goals! To practice visualization you must create a clean mental picture of the person you want to be or the result you want to get in life or in sales. You must see your goals achieved! This works because pictures and strong statements activate the subconscious mind. For example, when you say "I AM THE BEST!!!" you activate your subconscious mind to achieve excellence.

Servant Selling Concept #3 **Selling**

All top performers visualize; all poor ones don't! 95% of all sales people just wing it! All Pros warm up before entering the game. Visualization is mental warm up. Even the Bible says: Without Vision People Perish! Your vision is the blueprint of your life! You should practice positive visualization daily. Most people that say, "I don't believe in that visualization stuff" practice it all the time in the negative. Here's how: worry. Worry is negative use of visualization. You are seeing what you don't want happening in advance. It's kind of like this; fear is negative faith. Fear is actually faith in something harming you that has not happened yet. Faith is the image of good things not yet seen.

> *Visualization Develops Confident Expectation - Confident Expectation = Success.*

Confident selling is a positive challenge to the prospect. They start to think within themselves, this person is good at what they do. They are serious about selling automobiles. I wonder how cheap can I get out of here?

Chapter 10

"The Six Fundamentals of Selling"

*The people curse him who keeps grain for himself, but good comes to him who **sells** it.*
Ancient Hebrew Proverb

"Fundamentals win it. Football is two things: it's blocking and tackling. If you block and tackle better than the other team you will win."

Vince Lombardi

All Professional Selling Starts With Need Analysis!

Brian Tracy

There are simple fundamental principles involved in every professional sale. Here are some fundamentals to the Servant Selling sales process. Fundamental is defined as; basic, beginning, critical, essential, elementary, underpinning. I like the word *basic* because it reminds me of K.I.S.S! Fundamentals are simple basics of any art, and selling is an art. In fact, the fundamentals are transferable to most sales environments and products with a little adaptation to the product you are selling, if it is something other than automotive. For example, if you are selling vacuum cleaners you would not do a demo drive, however you would do a product demonstration. If you are selling real estate you would not do a trade evaluation, there is no trade. It is important for the student of this book to translate the fundamental to his/her product or service. Since a fundamental is also a basic step, I am going to call these fundamentals steps for simplicity.

"The Six Fundamentals of Selling"

STEP #1) NEED ANALYSIS

All professional selling starts with need analysis! Having a need is the main reason people buy a product. You job is to find a need and meet it! Of course, there are other reasons that people don't buy that you need to understand.   Oscar's good friend Zig Ziglar on his audio presentation, "Secrets of Closing the Sale", gave five basic reasons people don't buy a product or service: 1) no need, 2) no money, 3) no hurry, 4) no desire, 5) *no trust*

Notice that the fifth reason is no trust. Remember that trust accounts for fully 40% of the sale. Often you, as a salesperson, can do something about the trust factor.   A major trust factor is the concept of "The First Impression".

"You don't get a second chance to make a first impression!"

"The Six Fundamentals of Selling"

To make a positive first impression you must strive to be the professional sales person we discussed earlier.

Four First Impression Tips:
1.   Make eye contact immediately
2.   Communicate your sincerity
3.   A firm, enthusiastic handshake

Always remember the rule:

"People don't buy from people they don't like!"

Brian Tracy

"The Six Fundamentals of Selling"

To make a positive impression, it is critical that you develop rapport with the prospect. Here is some rapport building advice:

> **7 Keys To Establishing Rapport**
> 1. Respect For The Prospect
> 2. Don't Use High Pressure
> 3. Keep The Customer In The Spotlight
> 4. Ask Questions About Them
> 5. Make A Friend
> 6. Listen!!!
> 7. Seek To *Understand* The Prospect

After meeting a customer, making a positive first impression and building rapport is important to do need analysis.   To determine needs effectively, do a brief consultative interview:

1. Assure the customer that you are sincere.

2. Show the customer your concern.

3. Ask specific questions relating to their need:

"The Six Fundamentals of Selling"

In order to determine needs, it's important to understand the power of questions. Remember, **"Questions are the answer!"** Sally asked, "How many of you are skilled at asking questions." About ten percent of the class raised their hands. "Great, I have some simple, yet effective stuff on asking questions that will help." You must understand how to use two basic types of questions; first open-ended then closed-ended questions.

Servant Selling! © 2005 O. Bernard Smalls Companies   www.lulu.com/bernardsmalls

"The Six Fundamentals of Selling"

ASKING QUESTIONS SKILLFULLY

There are two basic types of questions that you must understand to be a successful Servant Seller. They are open-ended questions and closed-ended questions.

Open-ended questions are questions that are basically impossible for someone to answer yes or no. They will get you more information than closed-ended questions.

Here are some examples of open-ended questions:

What's important in a car to you?

Is there anything else I should know?

Closed-ended questions get you vital, but less information.

Such as:

Are you looking for a two or four door?

Do you want an automatic or manual transmission?

"The Six Fundamentals of Selling"

By now it was approaching 4: 00 PM, so Sally said, "I know we said we would go until 5:00 but I am going to give a break so that you remain Raving Fans of my training. You can leave now if you promise me that you will spend some time tonight memorizing the twelve steps to a sale." Everyone in the group stood up and gave Sally a standing O. As Joe was leaving he stopped and told Sally, "Throughout my career in software, I have never attended a better training class. I believe I can do this sales job and enjoy it. Thanks a million to you and Oscar for giving me a chance!"

"The Six Fundamentals of Selling"

HOME AGAIN!

As Joe pulled up, his ten-year-old daughter Jill was playing with a friend in the neighbor's yard. When she saw the BMW, she ran to meet him with an exuberant, "DADDY....you're home. How was work?" Joe said, "**FANTASTIC!** Where's mom?" "Oh, she went to the grocery store. She said she'll be right back. Her sister Janet is in the house doing some Internet research for a college exam."

About ten minutes later Jane walked in and said humorously, "Oh, I see Joe Girard. The greatest salesman ever has arrived." "Yes", said Joe. "How was it?" asked Jane. "Much better than I expected. The people were nice, the training room was great, and Sally the trainer – Jane, she is one of the best. I think we have found the solution to our financial challenge until the information technology crunch is over. You know, I might even consider a career in the auto business." "Boy, they must have impressed you." Joe said, "Yip, they sure did. What's for dinner? I'm so hungry I could eat a horse!"

"The Six Fundamentals of Selling"

The next morning Sally asked, "How many of you did your homework?" Eighty percent of the class, including Joe, raised their hands. Sally politely asked the rest of the class, "Why didn't you folks do the assignment?" One student said, "I was so busy I didn't get around to it." The rest of the students all agreed. Sally reached on the training table and picked up several sheets of paper that had the word **TUIT** in a circle. She smiled and gave them to the students that had not *gotten around to it* and said, "Now you have a **ROUND-TUIT!**" All of the recruits broke into either laughter or a smile. One of the students said, "We got it. I'll get around to it." Sally smiled and said, "You already have one!"

Sally explained the reason she gives out round-tuits. Action is a major key to success. In a seminar in Alaska, Peter J. Daniels, the Australian entrepreneur said, "Mastery of procrastination is the greatest tool to success! The number one reason for failure is putting off what you should do now." Sally added, "I agree whole-heartily. That's why I gave you the *round tuits* to get you moving. By the way, action oriented people are normally the top performers in a competitive sales environment."

"The Six Fundamentals of Selling"

"Now, let's get back into the fundamentals to sales success. Remember **Fundamental or Step # 1 is: Need Analysis or "Determine The Customers Needs."** This is also called the sales or consultative interview. I love what Zig Ziglar said in his book Secrets of Closing The Sale:

> *"On every <u>interview</u> a sale is made, either you sell the customer that they can and should buy, or they sell you that they can't and won't buy!"*

Note that the sale is made on the interview. This is critical. The sale is often made or lost in the consultative interview. Think deeply about this.

"The Six Fundamentals of Selling"

Sally then added, "All customers are ***just looking!*** They are just looking for a sales person they feel they can trust. Before you can discover needs and sell a car, you must sell yourself. Customers have inbred buyer's resistance so it is not always easy to determine their needs. When a customer says *I'm just looking* the customer is really saying; **I don't want you to give me a presentation that might make me want to buy yet.**

So, first you must close the customer on you as a win-win sales person and you will get information to determine their needs. In other words, when the customer likes you, trusts you, and respects you as a sales person she will give you more information about her real needs. Until then "I'm just looking" is a safety net to keep a Car Dawg out of her pocket. Your goal is to quickly prove that you are not just another Car Dawg! It's like when a kid meets a new dog. If the dog is friendly to the child, it's often the beginning of a win-win relationship." "Yeah", Joe said, "You got that right. My daughter Jill brings home every stray dog or cat in the neighbor if they are nice to her. I have warned of the potential of rabies but she won't listen."

"Good point, Joe. Customers are being warned in many ways in our information-based society about Car Dawgs. They don't want to get financial rabies or stuck with a lemon. Many states have even developed lemon laws to protect the consumer.

"The Six Fundamentals of Selling"

Also, remember that you begin closing when you meet the customer because you first close them on you as the right kind of person. Many still believe the old adage – "you can't make a good deal with a bad salesperson". Joe asked, "Are you saying the sales process is a continual closing process?" Oscar said, "Bingo, Joe. You got that right! A positive first impression will open the door for you determining the customer's needs. Generally speaking, **the customer must buy you before they buy your product.** Always remember, *"People don't buy from people they don't like!"*

"The Six Fundamentals of Selling"

Yesterday we said you must understand how to use two basic types of questions, first open ended then closed ended questions. Closed-ended questions get you vital but less information such as: Are you looking for a two or four door? Do you want a manual or automatic? Another powerful combination question would be: Are you looking for that in light or dark colors? This is what I call a combination question because it has some facets of both the open and closed ended question. The reason this is a powerful question is that if the customer says light or dark, you can accommodate them.

Sally said, "**NEVER ASK!!!! – WHAT COLOR DO YOU WANT?**" Sally asked, "How many of you have heard of Murphy's Law? Murphy's Law says if anything can go wrong, IT WILL!" Sally jokingly said, "Some people say that Murphy was an optimist! When you ask what color you want, you open the door to Murphy's Law." Joe raised his hand and asked, "Why Sally, why do you say that?" Sally replied, "Because in a negative world, the color they say they want is the color you won't have. Then you are stuck! And, once a customer tells you the color they want, it's tough to get them to change their mind.

"The Six Fundamentals of Selling"

In psychology, this is called cognitive dissonance: i.e. put in layman terms, **no healthy human likes to be wrong.** So, they will subconsciously fight to stay in control of the sales interview. If the say dark, you can show them an array of dark colors and chances are they will fall in love with one. Keep the playing field broad when it comes to color."

"The Six Fundamentals of Selling"

Repeat this question three times: **"Do you want that in a light or dark color?"** Either answer will give you as a sales person a range of color options to make available to the customer. For instance, if a customer says dark you can show the dark green, blue, black, charcoal, etc. The numbers tell us that 82% of people buy a car other than the car they left home intending to buy. I believe that this happens when they meet a professional salesperson.

You determine needs by asking questions skillfully.

Remember, *"Questions are the answer!"*

Sally asked the trainees, "What are some questions you would ask to determine a customers needs?" After they responded with several great questions Sally said, "Let's take ten, its break time."

CHAPTER 11

"The Six Fundamentals of Selling"
Step #2: PRESENTING F.A.B.

Features, Advantages & Benefits

"People are not going to give you a big stack of money for a small stack of benefits".   ***Zig Ziglar***

As the class returned from break, Sally asked, "How was the break?" "Great!" said Joe. "I got a little fresh air and saw a flock of Canadian Geese flying over in a nearly perfect V-formation. At my software company we had a Gung Ho! Seminar by a trainer from the Ken Blanchard Companies and they taught us why the geese fly that way for aerodynamic efficiency." "Great!" said Sally. "Oscar lives and breathes Ken Blanchard. Our organization uses lots of Ken's stuff. That guy is a genius."

Sally opened her training manual and said, "The next step in professional automobile sales is to do a feature/benefit presentation. **Don't forget that before attempting to do a feature benefit presentation, allow time to establish good rapport** or common ground. Remember that all of this training is based on the **friendship factor.**

Step #2: PRESENTING F.A.B. *Features, Advantages & Benefits*

Car Dawgs can care less about making friends with customers. In fact, they will call you weak if you admit that you practice relationship selling. They just want to ravage the money out of the customer, bite them with lies and deception, infect them with rabies, then rush them into finance where a Car Dawg of a different breed, the finance manager, tears into their flesh with 29.9% interest rates and inflated warranties. We want you to create a raving fan by making the customer feel like a king throughout the transaction! We have found that you make more money in the long run if you build lasting relationships with your customers.

Step #2: PRESENTING F.A.B. *Features, Advantages & Benefits*

What is a great customer relationship worth? I don't think you can measure it with monetary things! Any way, remember "He who pays the piper calls the tune!" It's crucial that you build rapport or establish common ground with the customer. People today don't want to be sold; they are looking for a friend. **Remember as I taught earlier, to understand your prospects, you need some basic understanding of the four personality types.** *You don't have to have a degree in psychology to be a great sales person; however there is much psychology involved in persuading the prospect to make a buying decision.*

Step #2: PRESENTING F.A.B. *Features, Advantages & Benefits*

Sally then said, "Oscar attended training in Minneapolis that trained him in four basic personality types. He later found that most research confirms the four basic personality types. I have also been trained to interpret the AVA that you completed before being hired. Big John asked, "Sally what does AVA mean again? Oscar told me during the interview but I let it slip." Sally responded, "No problem John. AVA stands for Activity Vector Analysis. It is a way of analyzing the vector (avenue) of personality. It tracks and locates your personality. In fact the AVA behavioral assessment was required to discover which of the four personality types you fit into.

The four vectors are 1) ASSERTIVENESS, 2) SOCIABILITY, 3) CALMNESS, and 4) CONFORMITY. Most effective sales people are high in vectors one and two. A student said, "That makes sense that a great sale person would be assertive and sociable. I imagine a timid introvert should not be in sales." Sally said, "You got that right! At least according to AVA. However, every once in a while a seemingly passive person, according to AVA, defies the odds and succeeds in sales. AVA is a behavioral science, a guide and not a hard science like math. In arithmetic, which is a hard science two plus two is always four. But the behavioral sciences have a lot of variables that must be factored in.

Step #2: PRESENTING F.A.B. *Features, Advantages & Benefits*

Let's take another look at DiSC.

D.i.S.C.

- **Dominant:** *aggressive, demanding*
- **Influencing:** *interact, people oriented*
- **Steady:** *cautious or calculating*
- **Compliant:** *yielding, conforming*

Step #2: PRESENTING F.A.B. *Features, Advantages & Benefits*

UNDERSTANDING THE CUSTOMER

Seek to understand the behavioral tendencies of the four personality types. Be aware of these behaviors. Use a sales strategy to help you in dealing with the different personality types. If your prospect has buying tendencies from more than one dimension, be flexible!

Of course, a **dominant** person would not want you to waste their time and to be specific. An **influencing** person, on the other hand, wants to have fun during the sales process. The **cautious** person would tend to be more analytical and careful about making the wrong decision. They are often research oriented. The **compliant** person is usually the easiest of the four to sell. But you will go broke trying to make a living on compliant people. You just won't meet that many.

Step #2: PRESENTING F.A.B. *Features, Advantages & Benefits*

Sally then said, "We must understand the art of DOING A PRESENTATION THAT BUILDS VALUE. I call it F.A.B.: Features, Advantages, and Benefits. You present a feature, describe the advantages, and then give the customer the benefits.

The presentation is what we call the "Walk Around" in the automobile sales business. Remember, people don't buy features they buy benefits. So, every time you present a feature, describe the benefit of the feature. This is why we call it a feature/benefit presentation.

Step #2: PRESENTING F.A.B. *Features, Advantages & Benefits*

DEMONSTRATION

Sally said, "Let's talk about what I call a critical success factor in selling any product or service. We call it demonstration. Demonstration is a part of presentation. In other words, you now demonstrate what you have presented. Demonstration means to show the prospect how the product works and what it will and can do.

In order to close more sales, you must demonstrate the vehicle by doing a demo drive with the customer. *Remember, people don't buy features, they buy benefits!"* Sally said, "Let's go to our training manuals and study the next section."

Step #2: PRESENTING F.A.B. *Features, Advantages & Benefits*

Selling is simple but it is important in integrity-based selling to help the customer decide if this is the right vehicle by demonstration. This also creates mental ownership for the customer. General Market Research of auto sales reveals that 99% of people surveyed said they would not buy a vehicle they had not test-driven. **Let's summarize F.A.B., or:**

How to do an Effective Presentation
- Conduct a customer needs assessment
- Make a recommendation
- Be client focused in the presentation
- Product comparison/advantages skills
- Demonstrate what you presented
- **Present with enthusiasm!!!**

Sally started to sing the old James Brown hit "I feel good da, da, da, da, da "and its break time – take ten.

CHAPTER 12
Six Fundamentals to a Sale
Step # 3: CLOSING

In servant/selling Oscar says it's not really closing the sale but RELATIONSHIP CLOSING that's important. Let me explain. When your heart is in your service and selling, your desire is to give the customer solutions. You actually open the sale by building a positive relationship. You must open the sale by building a relationship before you can close it and wrap up the order. Don't misunderstand me, we believe in closing. In fact, some people ask *when do you close*? I like what Zig Ziglar said in Secrets of Closing The Sale, *"You close early, you close late, you close all the time!"* Remember, it is relationship closing.

Let's take another quick look at Relationship Closing! You may ask, why look at relationship closing again? Because the sale stands or falls based on the relationship factor. Besides, *repetition is the mother of skill and the seed of learning.* First, you must understand that closing is the most stressful part of the sales relationship for the sales person and the customer.

Step # 3: CLOSING

Remember what I said earlier. The fear of failure is 80% of the reason the person refuses to make a buying decision. The fear of rejection is 80% of the reason that the sales person refuses to ask for the business.

Here are 4 Conditions that must be met in relationship closing:

> *The Customer needs it.*
> *The Customer can use it.*
> *The Customer can afford it.*
> *The Customer wants it.*

Here are 2 confirming questions before attempting to close: Do you have any questions or concerns I haven't covered? And, Does this make sense to you so far?

The sum of Servant Selling is: **"VALUE TO THE CUSTOMER"**

Step # 3: CLOSING

Since we are on a closing roll, let's cover in a snapshot the various kinds of closes used in Relationship Closing and then we will complete our sale discussion questions and take a lunch break.

6 KEY CLOSES

---

1. **The Directive Close** – *"if you have no further questions, then the next step is..."*

2. **The Authorization Close** – *"if you'll just authorize this, we'll get started right away."*

3. **Puppy Dog Close** – *let the prospect experience it.*

4. **The Order Sheet Close** – *write it up. The more information the closer you are to a sale.*

5. **The Abe Lincoln Close** – *argue both sides, but make yours stronger.*

6. **The Ben Franklin Close** – *draw a line, show the pros and cons. Helps the customer make the decision.*

The reason I gave you these specific closes is that you must overcome inbred buyer's resistance in regard to price. Practically everybody thinks the price is too high. *The reason is money represents freedom and we all want to maintain as much freedom as possible.*

Step # 3: CLOSING

Once a purchase is made our freedom to use that money is gone. This leads to procrastination, I need to think about it, sleep on it, and other "put it off" objections by the customer. To deal effectively with price you need to know the basics of negotiating.

Step # 3: CLOSING

THE ABC's OF NEGOTIATING

A- AVOID NEGOTIATING WHILE STANDING. NEVER NEGOTIATE ON THE LOT! It's tough to get control. The customer can easily walk away. They can wander around to keep you from pinning them down.

B- BE SEATED, AND HAVE THE CUSTOMER SIT. Negotiate from your position of power – seated at the desk. Relax! Keep the processes moving toward a buying decision. Assume the close! Once customers are inside and seated, always offer them a drink. Get the drink, and then start pulling out the necessary paperwork. Be proactive! Start doing the paperwork until the customer stops you. If the prospect doesn't stop you, just keep assuming the sale and completing the paperwork.

C- COMMUNICATE ON PAPER AND WITH WORDS. Use the buyer's work sheet as a talking pad. **People, particularly in the U.S., believe what they see and hear.** Keep assuming the close. Ask questions like:

"What address do you want on the registration?"

"Will this be in your name alone or your wife's also?"

Step # 3: CLOSING

Write the MSRP and additional packages on the buyer's order in BOLD PRINT. When negotiations start, <u>focus the customers' attention on the quality, trade-in value, and dependability of your product.</u>   If the customer mentions a competitor that's cheaper, express validity then kindly and respectfully ask, "Mr. Prospect, have you ever heard that *"Cheap products are seldom good, & good products are seldom cheap?"*

Step # 3: CLOSING

At Excellent Way, we believe in relationship negotiating. Let's check out the Purpose of Relationship Negotiating.

This concept has 3 Essential Parts:

1. To reach an agreement of some kind.

2. To assure that all parties are satisfied.

3. All parties are willing to negotiate again.

Relationship negotiating is designed to build a relationship that will last with the customer. Negotiating does not have to be a shouting match, or a circus.   Take a look at this: Win-Win or No Deal!   Let's talk about Relationship Negotiating vs. Hammering! Most so-called closers in the car business only know how to hammer.   They know little about true negotiating. I talked with a sales person at a dealership recently that could not get the customer to make a buying decision. She had the manager come out and talk to the customer. She said she counted as the manager asked the customer 12 times if he was going to buy a car or not? Seeing that he was getting nowhere, the manager asked the son four times.   If that isn't hammering, what is? Who in this room wants to be hammered by a Car Dawg? No hands went up.

Step # 3: CLOSING

The major keys to Servant Selling are <u>trust</u> and <u>credibility</u>.

Here are some of the key factors of Relationship Negotiating. Remember the challenge we have is one of building good relationships in a negotiating culture. Cars, for the most part, are negotiable. So, how do you build good relationships in a negotiating culture? Some dealers say it can't be done: *you better screw them before they screw you.* We have found it can be done if you understand the key factors. Example: you may not be able to fly a 747 aircraft, but don't say it can't be done. It happens everyday by pilots that have been trained to do it. It takes training to be good at relationship negotiating. Here are some of the critical steps:

- Listening builds trust. Lean forward and do not interrupt!
- Pause 3 to 5 seconds before replying.
- Consider carefully what the customer has said.
- Question for clarification. (Well prepared questions)

In relationship negotiating, skillful questions are the key!

Step # 3: CLOSING

10 Sample Relationship Negotiating Questions

1) What do you have in mind?

2) What else?

3) Do I know everything I should know…?

4) Is there another possibility?

5) What would it take to?

6) Is the offer clear?

7) What if or suppose that..?

8) Now that you have told me what you want…?

9) What do you need?

10) What's your offer?

Step # 3: CLOSING

Before we move into the next fundamental, let's discuss something that is a critical part of closing in a competitive market. **We call it competitive advantage or comparison.**

Always politely ask the prospect if they are shopping any other vehicles. If they say yes, ask: **what vehicles** are you considering? **Why**?

The reason is that you can present your competitive advantages. Sally said, "You must realize that Atlanta is one of the most competitive markets for automobiles in the world. Just look at the Saturday newspaper at the automotive section and it nearly blinds you, there are so many bait and switch ads.

Step # 3: CLOSING

Joe said, "I've heard that phrase before, but I don't understand exactly what it means." Sally said, "I'll gladly explain Joe. It's simply when a dealership puts a car in the paper priced below invoice (what they paid for it) to bait customers to come in. Then they change or switch you to a more expensive model because the one stock number in the paper at the low price is normally not for the car pictured in the ad but for one that did not have air conditioning and is a polka-dot five speed with roll up windows and only an A.M. Radio. Many smart customers see those ads and immediately say, *that is too good to be true.*

Sally said, "We operate in integrity based selling at our dealership, but buyers everywhere are often taken in by the bait and switch tactics of the ravishing Car Dawgs. Now, back to compare shopping. Since most vehicles are negotiable, customers in general will shop! Who doesn't want the best deal in today's marketplace?

Step # 3: CLOSING

Here are some keys for dealing with a bona-fide shopper:

- **Make a friend!** The Car Dawgs will make an enemy 99% of the time when a customer says they are going to shop around before buying. Greedy Car Dawgs only think of selling now. They immediately call the shopper a tire-kicker in their own mind and they start to treat them like one. *"People don't buy from people they don't like."*
- **Realize that most people don't want to shop, but they don't want to be ripped off either, so they will.** Ask the customer kindly: Sir, if you like the person, (me) the place (our dealership) and the product (our car), why shop anywhere else?
- **Show your competitive advantages.** Use the three P's to demonstrate your competitive advantage: P - Person (You), P - Place (Your dealership), P - Product and your Products advantages.
- **Never put down the competition!** Be complementary! – For example: if the customer says I'm going to look at Honda. Say, Honda is a fine product. However, here is what we found, and give the competitive advantages of your product. Remember, when you slam the competition the customer grabs his wallet and tries to exit! In servant selling, you want what is best for the customer.

Step # 3: CLOSING

- **Build more value in your place of business** – our competitive advantages at our particular dealership. It could be as simple as the location. Sometimes people will drive 50 miles away from home to buy a car. But, who wants to go that far away for service? Try to tie in service with the sale by offering some small concession that is valuable to the customer. You would be amazed at what "FREE" oil changes for the first year would do to build value in our dealership.

Step # 3: CLOSING

Sally repeated a story that Oscar often tells:

    " I lived in Alaska and worked for a large General Motors dealership where we had little to no real competition. So, shopping was not a major issue. Either you bought from us or you drove sixty miles (on ice and snow 8 months of the year) to our competitor that had a very limited inventory. But when I moved to Atlanta I was shocked at how people would shop from dealership to dealership to save a few bucks.   At one point there were seventeen Toyota dealerships in driving distance.   People would literally shop till they dropped!"

    Here is a personal tip that is helpful for making more sales in a shoppers market. It is called "The walk away close". It works like this. First, when the customer wants to shop, give them a good reason for not shopping. Second, if they insist, use *"Today Only"* and give them a great incentive for buying today. This will not apply any other time.

    Joe said, "Wait a minute, Sally. That seems a little car dawgie to say today only." Sally said, "This sounds like a slick trick unless you give the customer a real, specific reason for offering him today only. Here are some examples: today is the last day of the rebate, the last day of the sale, or today is the last day of the month and we need to sell this car to help hit our monthly objective.

Step # 3: CLOSING

If you don't give an intelligent reason the customer will probably resent "today only!" Joe said, "I guess what you are saying is you create urgency by using real reasons for buying today versus lies and gimmicks." Sally said, "You got it, Joe."

The key is to make sure it's true and not a gimmick. Peter Daniels calls it THE POWER OF PERSUASION WITH THE HONESTY FACTOR!

Step # 3: CLOSING

Finally, Sally said, if they persist, tell them to go with a promise to come and see you before they buy, and that you will give them the best deal in town. Sally then asked the class to answer the discussion questions before they took lunch. She said, "It's just about lunchtime and, by the way, Joe is buying!" Joe said, "No way Jose! Not yet. Let me get a few sales under my belt first and get a fat (fat) *check*." Sally said, "I was just joking Joe." -:)

CHAPTER 13

Six Fundamentals to a Sale

Step #4: GETTING REFERRALS

The poor man is hated even by his neighbor, but the rich man has many friends.
Ancient Hebrew Proverb

Sally arrived back into the class forty-five minutes later with a Starbuck's venti vanilla latte. She noticed that five people were already there ready to go. She asked, "Didn't you guys go to lunch?" A young lady said, "Yeah, but we are enjoying this training so much we got back early to get a front row seat!" "Funny!" said Sally. "Well it's been an hour. Let's get started. Oscar often quotes Ben Franklin who said: *Don't waste time it's the stuff life is made of*!"

Let's talk about getting referrals. The best way to get referrals is to create raving fans out of the prospects you serve. When you create a raving fan, you actually make a friend of your prospect. I call it friendship selling. If you give excellent service, people will talk and even brag about you to others and you will automatically get referrals.

Step #4: GETTING REFERRALS

How many of you talk about a great restaurant you have visited to your friends, family, and associates? Why? Because it was so good, we just want to share. The same is true about service. Great service is so rare today that when you deliver it, people will talk about it.

I want to again share Ken Blanchard's Three Secrets to Excellent Customer Service. (For customer service excellence, see the author's book – Thank God It's Sunday; The Gospel of Customer Service); three secrets to providing outstanding customer service as taught in Raving Fans.

Step #4: GETTING REFERRALS

Sally asked the class, "What is the mother of skill?" They all said in unison, "Repetition!" "OK, let's repeat the three secrets of creating raving fans."

Secret #1: Determine what you want! "You can get whatever you want in life if you help enough people get what they want". Think about your personal, financial, family, and career goals. Develop a winning vision for your life and sales career; a vision centered on perfection based on customer benefits. You must have a vision of customer service excellence!

Secret #2: Find out what the customer wants! Learn to listen to the customer! So often we are not selling based on the customers values. Here is a practical formula; ask questions 20% of the time & listen 80% of the time. Car Dawgs tell more than they ask because they don't know that "When you are asking questions you are in control!"

Secret #3: Deliver More than You Promise! Close the gap between promise and practices. Liars are always promising customers the world just to make a sale. Then they make excuses and never deliver because the customer is now the owner of the car. A sales pro always delivers plus 1%! Delivery must be consistent at all times. The vision and what you are actually doing becomes one.

Servant Selling! © 2005 O. Bernard Smalls Companies www.lulu.com/bernardsmalls

Step #4: GETTING REFERRALS

Sally then summarized by saying the long and short of it is: **"Always deliver more than you promise and you will get referrals!"** Sales people must also learn to ask for referrals from the people they sell and serve. That seems obvious, but many sale people never do. Here is what I do:

1) Deliver awesome service consistently.

2) Ask the people I serve for referrals consistently.

There is one caveat to getting referrals. You must focus the customers' attention to a specific group of people by asking: who do you know at your Church that is looking for, or in need of, my product or service? Now the prospect will think specifically about people at Church and narrow the focus to come up with several names.

K.I.S.S. *Keep It Simple Students!*

Step #4: GETTING REFERRALS

If you just say *who do you know that is looking for a new car*, this is too global. The customer will tend to not come up with anyone because they are not focused on a specific group. This is because of the R.A.S. (reticular activator system) in the human brain, which notices what it is reminded of. For example, if you go and look at a certain car you are considering buying, have you noticed that you then start seeing that car everywhere? That's because you focused on one particular car and now your brain starts to eliminate the cars you are not interested in. The same is true in getting referrals. You can help your customer activate his R.A.S. Joe said to Sally, "Heavy, heavy stuff!" Sally said, "Thank you Joseph! Let's stand up and take a break."

Step #4: GETTING REFERRALS

After lunch Sally said, "Since we had some a sumptuous lunch, I know this afternoon session may be a little tough. Here is what I want you to do instead of sitting in here on such a beautiful day. I am going to give you some time to go out and shop the competition." Big John asked, "What? Shop another dealership?" "That's right", said Sally. "The reason we do this is for you to compare notes on what you are hearing in here and what you see out there so that you learn by precept and example. You should act like a customer wanting to look at and drive a car that you are considering purchasing." Joe said, "This is going to be fun, fun, fun! I know what I want to drive already..."

Sally said, "I want you to pick a partner so that you go two by two. This makes it easier for someone that's a little gun-shy and you can feed off of each other's questions. After you have done the shopping, you can do whatever you want to for the rest of the afternoon." Obbie said, "Sally you are the greatest. I don't care what they say about you." Sally smiled and dismissed the class as she rang the bell on her old fashioned cooking timer.

Step #4: GETTING REFERRALS

Joe and his shopping partner, Obbie, both left on cloud nine! Joe said, "Obbie, this is an occasion for a sugar-free vanilla latte." Obbie said, "I am all in.   Let's do it."   He pulled his BMW into Starbucks with great excitement. He walked in whistling and popping his fingers. The girl at the counter said, "Boy, you came in smiling like you walked through a swinging door on someone else's push."   Joe said, "It's been an awesome day." He ordered his coffee, paid for Obbie's, and left a five dollar tip!

"Thanks Joe! That's generous of you." said the girl. "Yeah, I have a new gig at Excellent Way Automotive Group and I am about to make Big Bucks. So, I may as well start acting like it." Joe and Obbie went to the nearest Toyota dealership and had fun shopping the competitor.

CHAPTER 14

Six Fundamentals to a Sale
Step # 5: FOLLOW UP!

Lazy hands make a man poor, but **diligent** hands bring wealth.
Ancient Hebrew Proverb

If you want to truly be successful in sales, be diligent in follow up!
Why? Because most people will not buy on the first visit. In our industry, if you have a 20% closing ratio you are doing great. That means if you talk to 100 people, 20 of them bought on the first visit. That leaves 80 to follow up on. What you do with those 80 people month after month will determine your long-term success as sales professional.

Why follow-up? Here are three powerful reasons:

1) Follow-up is a good customer service practice.

2) Follow-up increases referral business.

3) Follow-up creates customers for life!

Sally enunciated, "Research reveals that approximately 80% of people that leave a car dealership never receive a follow up call or letter from the sales person. I believe that follow up is critical!

Step # 5: FOLLOW UP!

"Let's look at one more power-point slide before we break for a good lunch. By the way," Sally asked, "Who's buying?" No hands went up. "Just kidding guys. There is a new Cajun restaurant called Papa-Joe's. Oscar has made reservations for the whole class to go have lunch on him today." The whole class started to cheer, whistle, clap, and so forth. Big John said, "Lets' go now. I'm so hungry I could eat a horse!" Obbie jokingly said, "I hope Oscar has his gold American Express card paid up." Big John said, "Watch it now!" as he winked at Obbie.

Sally hurriedly said, "FOLLOW UP! Repeat it 3 times." The class said, **"FOLLOW UP! FOLLOW UP! FOLLOW UP!"**

Step # 5: FOLLOW UP!

---

5 KEYS TO FOLLOW UP

1. See yourself as the follow up king/queen.

2. Use the phone. Approximately 20 % get a call after leaving a dealership. When you call it makes you unique to the prospect.

3. Use the mail. Write thank you note to buyers and non-buyers.

4. Be organized. Have a system that let's you know who you have or have not called.

5. Contact the customer within 24 hours of every sales interview. Whether they buy or not.

"Since follow up is so, so, important I want to give you a gift I call RICH follow up." Sally picked up a stack of handouts from the training table and started to pass them around. "This will help you execute your follow-up call with excellence. When doing a follow up call, it is crucial to have a strategy.

Step # 5: FOLLOW UP!

RICH follow-up gives you a strategy. Here is how it works. RICH is an acronym for:

- **R – Restate the outcome of the first visit**
- **I – Isolate the reason they didn't buy**
- **C – Convert the reason into another appointment**
- **H – Handle the objection on the next visit.**   Maybe by doing another demonstration and getting the customer a better price if possible.

Diligent follow-up can make you rich because it gets the customer in again for you to make your offer and attempt to close! Call them until they Buy or Die! *You can get rich by doing RICH follow-up!*

Step # 5: FOLLOW UP!

Joe said, "Sally, that was great stuff! When I think I have heard it all, you just keep pouring it on. I can see myself as the follow-up king of the whole hill." "If you get RICH, you'll get rich by enriching the lives of your prospect with relationship follow-up. The reason I call it relationship follow-up is that is what FORM is all about: building a relationship that will last through professional selling. Sally said, "Let's take a ten minute break and then I want to share with you one of the most powerful things Oscar ever taught me about accepting myself which has lead to enormous success in my sales career."

CHAPTER 15
Six Fundamentals Steps to a Sale
STEP #6: PROSPECTING

seek and you will **find...** Matthew 7:

Sally said, "We are reaching the end of the trail. Let's share the basics of prospecting. Prospecting is important! Always be asking – where is my next sale coming from? Prospecting literally means to find customers the way the old fashioned prospector would find gold. Let's look at poor versus good prospects. Look at the screen please:

<u>**Poor Prospects!**</u>

Characteristics:

- Sees little benefit in what you offer.
- Difficult, negative personality.
- Argues continually about price.
- Not a good source of referrals.

STEP #6: PROSPECTING

Good Prospects!

Characteristics:

· A real need for what you are selling.

· Power and authority to make a buying decision.

· Likes you, your company and your product.

· Can be a multiplier if happy.

· Is a center of influence opening doors for other prospects.

9 Sure-Fire Prospecting Keys

1. Hand out 20 business cards daily.

2. Contact sold customers monthly and offer bird dogs.

3. Work the service drive.

4. Mail hot letters (hot prospects)

5. Mail cold letters.

6. Join the local chamber of commerce.

7. Write select business people introducing yourself.

8. Ask for referrals each time you make a sale.

9. Read; How to Win Friends & Influence People. (Dale Carnegie)

STEP #6: PROSPECTING

PERSONAL WORKSHOP

•How many business cards will you hand out weekly? Why?

_____

_____

_____

•What will you do to increase the business card action? Why?

_____

_____

_____

•What organization(s) can you join to network for more sales?

_____

_____

_____

CHAPTER 16
Self Concept

I looked everywhere for the enemy, to the north, south, east and west and ...finally I found that the enemy was within-a-me!"

Willie Jolley

Sally opened the class with a hearty good morning and had a wonderful review session with all of the trainees asking and answering questions during the first session. After a short break, the class returned to find beef jerky, mixed nuts, and a variety of fresh fruit sitting on the refreshment counter. Most of the men went for the jerky while the ladies moved in on the fresh fruit. Sally said, "Please eat as much as you want since this is the last training session. I don't want any leftovers.

As they were chomping on their goodies, Sally said, "Since this is my final day with you in training, I want to share a story about a sales superstar and how he discovers the power of self-concept in relation to sales. Oscar, our owner, was a high performing sales person who learned and understood the value of cashing in on self-concept! I want to show you the power of self-concept as it relates to the psychology of selling by sharing Oscar's success."

SELF CONCEPT

Oscar learned by reading, that self-concept affects every area of life. It is like looking into a mirror and seeing an image that will manifest in the material world. Oscar knew that in sales, you never earn more outwardly than you do inwardly. Oscar, through visiting the motivational and sales section on the bookstore frequently, learned that developing a healthy self-concept is often a struggle because we live in a negative world. He discovered that most people see the proverbial cup as half empty rather than half full.

SELF CONCEPT

In his research, Oscar found that there are six areas of selling. Strengthening your self-concept is in each area of selling = more competence. One way Oscar increased his self esteem was to say over and over *I like myself.* This is called positive self-talk in the realm of applied behavioral sciences. He learned that saying *I like myself* over and over impressed the words into his subconscious mind. When he was asked by the manager to share the secret of his success in a sales meeting, he absolutely waxed eloquent. With enthusiasm and energy, he told the sales team how the subconscious believes what you say about yourself; hence self-esteem is enhanced. As you begin to see yourself as a big winner in sales through developing a healthy self-concept, your income is bound to go up.

SELF CONCEPT

If you adopt and live by three simple rules of **Servant Selling** you will sell more in today's market:

3 Simple Rules of Servant Selling
1. Do what is right.
2. Do the best you can do.
3. Treat people the way you would like to be treated!

Oscar developed his self-concept as a sales person and now he is the owner of the world's greatest automobile dealership, EXCELLENT WAY Automotive. Sally said, "Let's take a break and when we get back I want to teach you what Ken Blanchard shared about customer service and profits in his wonderful book **Big Bucks** – How to Make Serious Money. Ken really teaches us how to hear KACHING!"

BIG BUCKS

After the break Sally gave out the outlines entitled: Big Bucks! How to Hear KACHING in Sales. Let's take a look at the outline:

FOUR TESTS YOU MUST PASS TO MAKE BIG BUCKS!
#1:   The Test of Joy/Fun!

Being positive and excited about your work! Business takes place when the customer is excited about using the product! Fun means being turned on when a customer enjoys your product or service! *This focus comes from a real love for the business. Then, work becomes enjoyable and becomes play.* Ray Kroc, who built McDonald's, could talk hours about a French fry. He was a fanatic for cleanliness. He loved restaurants and was having fun. Through the grind, the hours, and the challenges of the car biz, – the business must be fun! Fun is when WORK becomes PLAY. People who know the secrets of making money naturally enjoy L.U.C.K.: Laboring Under Correct Knowledge.

BIG BUCKS

#2:   The Test of Purpose!

Develop a sharp making money focus. **You can't make money unless making money is more important than having fun!** The Fun of Making Money is more important than the Fun of Doing Business! You must take making money seriously. It must be the top priority of your business career. Unless intensity comes first, you find you are just playing games. Unless intensity is matched with money making as a top priority, you won't have the drive - or the right goal - to be a successful money-maker.

Energy and Discipline: once you've achieved that necessary energy by having fun, it has to be disciplined and directed – that is what PURPOSE is all about. You don't add excitement and energy to focus; you add focus to excitement and energy! Fun is a time priority. Making Money is a strategic priority.

BIG BUCKS

#3:   The Test of Creativity!

Break out of the HERD mentality.   Creativity Defined – originality, ingenuity, resourcefulness, and vision.   Creative thinking is the highest function of the human mind. You can THINK AND GROW RICH!

The Creative Person: Seven Characteristics You Can Develop:

1. He realizes his mind is a storehouse that must be restocked.
2. He has a carefully sought out set of goals.
3. He desires to live an uncommon life.
4. He regularly thinks creatively about his work.
5. He respects the minds of others.
6. He avoids prejudice and close-mindedness.
7. He expects to win.

BIG BUCKS

#4:   The Test of Perpetual Prosperity!

Build a castle through relationships with customers that buy from you so that they come back again and again! KACHING! This process is critical because customers are more educated and knowledgeable about products and services than ever before. And, they are looking for a salesperson they can trust. When the customer allows the relationship to continue, you have earned their trust. **Service builds the bridge of trust.** I believe that we should provide outstanding customer service for our guests that are in the market for automobiles. SET A GOAL TO HAVE EVERY CUSTOMER COMPLETELY SATISFIED! The right mental attitude toward customer service is: Perfection is my goal!

Sally then gave the class a test on what they had studied in training. They graded each other's papers in class and everyone passed it with flying colors. "Now that you have completed the course, I have something for you from Oscar Paywell."

Oscar's assistant came in with a small gift for each student with a beautiful certificate of completion. The class was thrilled. They said they also had something for the teacher. One of the students got up and went behind the wall and came back with a Nordstrom gift bag with three different expensive ladies colognes, a box of Godiva chocolates and two beautiful silk scarves. Sally's eye filled with tears as she said, "WOW! This is too much guys. You spent a mint and I can't accept these gifts." The class said, "You must." Sally quickly grabbed the bag and said, jokingly, but seriously, "OK, you have persuaded me."

Sally walked the class around the facilities to show them where everything was and how the process of sales worked. She introduced them to managers and others as they went. She said, "Well guys, you've seen the layout of the facilities and inventory, so I will take you to Jeff, the sales manager and he will give you your schedule and pair you up with an experienced salesman so that you can piggyback, or shadow, for a week for some practical OJT before you are fully released to the sales floor. Remember, tomorrow is Saturday and the sales meeting is at 8:00 sharp tomorrow morning. Don't be late! Oscar will be there and it will be exciting!"

CHAPTER 17

Success Motivation For Sales People

On Saturday morning, the new trainees attended their first EXCELLENT WAY Saturday Kick-Off sales meeting. The music was thumping and the place was jumping! Balloons, confetti, and laughter filled the room. Oscar was there and he would be conducting the meeting.

After a time of social interaction, Oscar went up to the platform. He gave out cash bonuses, plaques, tee-shirts and all as they enjoyed a wonderful, sumptuous, breakfast. He welcomed the new team members and told all of the sales staff, "I have a motivational gift for you today. I call it *Sales Meetings In a Can!* It is a book of sales meetings so that you can have your own little sales seminar any day of the week. This way you don't have to wait for Saturday. You could call it Daily Success Motivation for Sales People. Why SUCCESS MOTIVATION for Sales People?
I have heard many sales people over the years say; Saturday is my money day – Thank God it's Saturday! Why?"

In many traditional selling situations, Saturday is a huge retail day. In my years as a corporate trainer, I have truly discovered that SUCCESS ATTITUDES Motivate Sales People to Win Everyday, not just Saturday. In other words, sales people need a daily check up from the neck up to have sustained sales growth and make Big Bucks and continually hear KACHING!

SUCCESS MOTIVATION FOR SALES PEOPLE

After Oscar had given the book to the sales team, he had them turn to the lesson **"7 Habits of Highly Defective Salespeople."**

7 HABITS OF HIGHLY DEFECTIVE SALES PEOPLE

Seven Reasons Sales People Fail

#1 They have a losing attitude!
"You generally get what you expect out of life."

#2 They quit growing!
"You are what you are because of what's gone into your mind."

#3 They have no game plan for life!
Vision without action = daydream.
Action without vision= nightmare.

#4 They are unwilling to change!
"Some people would rather cling to what they hate rather than embrace what might be better."

#5 They fail continually in relationships!
"People who cannot get along with others never get ahead in life."

#6 They are unwilling to sacrifice for success!
"The road to success is uphill all the way…"

#7 Failure to follow up on customers!
Most sales people fail because they fail to follow up!

Remember;

71% OF PEOPLE BUY FROM YOU BECAUSE THEY LIKE YOU, TRUST YOU, AND RESPECT YOU!

After sharing this powerful motivational speech, Oscar gave out the awards to top performers and gave out lots of cash and sent his Gung-Ho sales team out to have a great weekend! Each of the new students had at least one sale that day. At the end of the day Joe asked Obbie how he had done and Obbie said, "I sold 2! Man this is fun." Joe said, "Yeah, I sold 2 also and one was the biggest deal of the day for the whole dealership. Thank God for Oscar and Sally and for Servant Selling!"

K.I.S.S!
Keep
It
Simple
Students!

Chapter 18

How To Increase Your Income

*There is one who scatters, yet **increases** more; And there is one who withholds more than is right, But it leads to poverty.*

Wealth gained by dishonesty will be diminished, But he who gathers by labor will increase.

Ancient Hebrew Proverbs

Hi! I'm Oscar Bernard Smalls. I hope you have enjoyed Servant Selling. I want to close it with a gift to you, a teaching called HOW TO INCREASE YOUR INCOME. No matter the product or service you sell, you can experience increase by following the principles of this special report.

Did you know that only 3% of our nation's population has an income exceeding 100K? Are you one of them, or are you in the 97% that seem to struggle to get by, year after year, just paying your lousy bills? If you are not one of the 3%, my first goal is to get you into the top 3%. If there is so much abundance in our world and God wants us to be rich, then why are so few wealth in our abundant, free-enterprise society? My experience and research has shown me that only about 2% - 3% understand the "Law of Abundance."

HOW TO INCREASE YOUR INCOME

For example, study after study reveals that only 2% - 3% of our society has clearly defined goals. The amazing thing is that same 2% - 3% is worth more financially than the remaining 97% combined. Most people have the ability to earn twice as much as they are earning right now. To earn more, you must understand the "Law of Abundance." The law of abundance is: we live in an abundant universe in which there is sufficient money for all who really want it and are operating by the laws governing increase.

> *"If you took a hundred economists and laid them all head to feet, they would not even reach a conclusion."*
>
> **Peter J. Daniels**

The Good Report is:

YOU CAN HAVE ALL YOU WANT

There is plenty of money available to you. There is no real shortage. God has placed us in a generous universe and we are surrounded on all sides by blessings and abundant opportunities to acquire all we truly desire. The truth is "God wants You Rich!" Your attitude, either of abundance or scarcity, will have a major impact on whether you become rich or not.

HOW TO INCREASE YOUR INCOME

ECONOMY OR ECONO-ME?

Many are saying they cannot enjoy abundance because of the present economy. The economy is really a state of mind - your mind. People with attitudes and actions of abundance will thrive and prosper in spite economy. I call it ECONO-ME: my economy is on the account of ME! The economy is either good or bad right between your two ears. Remember that even during the great depression, many Americans got very rich!

When asked, "What would you do if you lost all of your wealth?" Australian millionaire Peter J. Daniels said, "I would find something to sell, because commission sales people are the highest paid people in the world and commission is set for mediocrity - any fool can beat mediocrity!" Yes, selling could be your ticket to financial increase. With proper training and renewed thinking, most people can make a great living in sales. Why? People will buy what they really need in good or bad times.

"As a man thinks in his heart, so is he (and his economy)."

HOW TO INCREASE YOUR INCOME

9 KEYS TO INCREASING YOUR INCOME

1.   MAKE A DECISION

The first law of abundance says that people become wealthy because they decide to become wealthy. They become wealthy because they believe they have the ability to become wealthy. Because they believe it completely, they act accordingly. "According to your faith, be it unto you." They consistently take the necessary actions that turn their dreams into realities. You can always tell what your beliefs are by looking at your actions. There is no other way. People are poor because they have not decided to become wealthy.

2.   EXAMINE YOUR THINKING

In the book, *The Instant Millionaire* by Mark Fisher, the old millionaire asks the boy who had so much advice about becoming a millionaire, "Why aren't you already rich?"

This is an important question to ask yourself. However you answer this question will reveal a lot about your financial condition. Your answer will expose your self-limiting beliefs, your doubts, your fears, your excuses, your rationalizations and your justifications.

HOW TO INCREASE YOUR INCOME

3.   **REVIEW YOUR REASONS**

Why aren't you already rich? Write down all of the reasons you can think of. Go over your answers with someone who knows you well and ask them their opinion. You may be surprised to find that most of your reasons are excuses that you have fallen in love with. Whatever your reasons or excuses, you can get rid of them NOW. The world is full of people who have had far greater difficulties to overcome than you could ever imagine and have gone on to be wealthy and successful. So can you.

4.   **The 20 IDEA METHOD**

The twenty idea method can turn any financial situation around if applied to the problem properly. Here's how it works. Think of your most pressing financial problem and write it down clearly. Be very specific. No problem can be intelligently solved until succinctly identified. Now think! Make your brain come up with 20 ideas or solutions to the financial problem. You will be amazed at the quality of ideas that come out of you as you persist. The 20 idea method is a tool for creative thinking. Creative ideas are the source of wealth.

HOW TO INCREASE YOUR INCOME

5.   PUT KEY IDEAS INTO ACTION

Action is the key! "DO IT NOW" are three of the most powerful words for success. Ideas are of little worth if you don't act on them. Take the top five ideas from your 20 idea list and spend some quiet time thinking on these. Out of the top five, choose the top three. Out of the top three, select the top one to act on NOW. Take massive action on this idea today. Your life will never be the same when you start acting on your key ideas.

6.   VALUE SMALL BEGINNINGS

Small efforts often yield large results! The good news is that even a small effort on your part to implement the very best ideas into your life will yield a tremendous return in increase productivity, performance and prosperity. It's like stepping on the accelerator in a car: this small action gets you moving big time. Small beginnings can get you on the financial fast track in 2004.

HOW TO INCREASE YOUR INCOME

7.   **EDUCATE FOR EFFICIENCY**

We live in a changing world. To keep up with the changes in the 21st Century, you must commit to continuous education. The word that made Japan a super-power is "kaizen" which means - constant and continuous improvement through small changes. To improve continuously you must continually upgrade your mind. Learn every thing you can. Attend every seminar, order self-improvement tapes, books and personal development material every chance you get. Become a student of the game. Efficiency often starts at school. The thought that school is just for the young is a myth. Learn everything you can in relation to your mission in life. Make a commitment to education and sophistication.

8.   **BE AN EXCELLENT WORKER**

Most people are poor workers! According to studies, fully 50% of adults could not work a full day if their life depended on it. They simply cannot stay on task! They are continually diverted and distracted into idle socializing, personal problems, shooting the breeze, arriving late, leaving early, taking too much time on lunch and coffee breaks and the beat goes on... The same people often wonder why they are not promoted and entrusted with increased responsibilities and more income.

You must be worth more to be paid more, and developing an excellent work ethic is still a major key to more income.

HOW TO INCREASE YOUR INCOME

9.   GET PROMOTED FASTER AND PAID MORE

The fact is, if you do an excellent job in a timely fashion, you cannot help but be paid more and get promoted faster. We live in a meritocracy. In a meritocracy, you are rewarded purely on the basis of the valuable contribution you make to the lives and work of others.

I believe that if you commit to diligently applying these nine principles, and the principles of **Servant Selling,** you will experience more increase. There are no glass ceilings and no barrier to your advancement!

Chapter 19

The Beginning!

Yeah! You say, but this is the end, not the beginning! I submit to you that it's not the end, but the beginning! As you digest and apply the principles and concepts you have learned in Servant Selling – Selling Made Simple, you will see that it is the beginning of super success in sales and life because you are now ready to start operating as a STEWARD, SERVANT and SELLER! WOW! That's good.

First, thanks again for reading my book. My sincere prayer is that this book will bring you the understanding and financial success you deserve. You may even consider starting a small group and using this book as the text for your weekly breakfast or lunch as you study a chapter each week with a group of sales people or like-minded business associates. If this book has helped you, I ask you to share it with at least one other person.

May you continue to increase financially more and more as you operate as a steward, servant, and seller and continually operate in the concepts of *SERVANT SELLING!*

AT YOUR SERVICE,

Bernard

Bibliography

The Psychology of Selling - Brian Tracy

Secrets of Closing the Sale –Zig Ziglar

Mastering the Art of Selling – Tom Hopkins

Selling Your Services– Robert W. Bly

GenderSell –Judith C. Tingley & Lee E. Robert

Speak & Grow Rich – Dottie Walters

Raving Fans – A revolutionary approach to customer service – Ken Blanchard & Sheldon Bowles

Big Bucks! – Ken Blanchard & Sheldon Bowles

"Not so with you. Instead, whoever wants to become great among you must be your **servant**, and whoever wants to be first must be your slave— just as the Son of Man did not come to be served, but to **serve**, and to give his life as a ransom for many."

Jesus

Who is Bernard Smalls?

O. BERNARD SMALLS IS ONE OF THE MOST ENTHUSIASTIC PUBLIC SPEAKERS AND TRAINERS IN THE WORLD TODAY. HIS SPEECHES ARE FILLED WITH PRACTICAL WISDOM AND INSPIRATION.

MR. SMALLS, HIS WIFE KAREN, AND THEIR FOUR CHILDREN RESIDE IN ATLANTA, GEORGIA, WHERE THEY HAVE FOUNDED FOUNDING CONCEPTS, A *TOTAL MAN* TRAINING AND DEVELOPMENT CENTRE.

BERNARD HAS WORKED IN SEVERAL KEY MANAGEMENT POSITIONS IN THE CORPORATE ARENA AND IN THE NON-PROFIT SECTOR. THOSE WHO KNOW HIM HAVE AFFECTIONATELY CALLED HIM THE "GUNG HO GURU".

BERNARD HAS DONE CONSULTING, SPEAKING, AND TRAINING FOR **THE UNITED STATES BANKRUPTCY COURTS, JOB CORPS OF AMERICA, BOOTSTRAPS OF AMERICA, ALLTEL COMMUNICATIONS, AMERICAN SOCIETY OF TRAINING AND DEVELOPMENT,** AND MORE. HE IS ALSO THE VISITING LECTURER TO SEVERAL COLLEGES IN THE ATLANTA AREA, WHILE COMPLETING HIS BACHELORS DEGREE IN PHILOSOPHY OF THEOLOGY.

BERNARD MAJORS IN HUMAN BEHAVIOR AND TRAINING IN THE AREA OF "HUMAN PERFORMANCE SYSTEMS." HE HAS COMPLETED COURSES IN SITUATIONAL LEADERSHIP FOR MANAGERS AND TRAINING FOR TRAINERS WITH **"THE KEN BLANCHARD COMPANIES",** DISC – DIMENSIONS IN HUMAN BEHAVIOR TRAINING WITH THE CARLSON LEARNING CENTER, AND HE IS A CERTIFIED "EXECUTIVE ACTIVITY VECTOR ANALYST" AUTHORIZED TO ADMINISTER THE AVA BEHAVIORAL ASSESSMENTS. HAVING STUDIED THEOLOGY AND THE BEHAVIORAL SCIENCES HIS TRAININGS AND SPEECHES ARE FILLED WITH INSPIRATION AND POSITIVE MOTIVATION.

BERNARD IS THE CORPORATE TRAINER FOR THE "WORLD CLASS" TOYOTA MALL OF GEORGIA IN ATLANTA, GEORGIA. BY TRAINING HUNDREDS OF THE EMPLOYEES IN THE RAVING FANS PHILOSOPHY HE SHARED IN THEIR RECORD SETTING SUCCESS BY **MAKING TOYOTA HISTORY, WINNING ALL 10 OF THE PRESTIGIOUS CUSTOMER SERVICE EXCELLENCE** AWARDS TOYOTA MOTOR CORPORATION INTERNATIONAL OFFERS IN THE FIRST YEAR OF BUSINESS, A FEAT THAT HAS NEVER BEFORE BEEN ACCOMPLISHED ANYWHERE IN THE WORLD, THUS MAKING HISTORY!

MR. SMALLS WAS ASKED IN SEPTEMBER OF 1999 BY DR. KEN BLANCHARD TO BECOME A CONSULTING RESOURCE PARTNER WITH THE LEGENDARY CO-AUTHOR OF THE "ONE MINUTE MANAGER, THE BEST SELLING BUSINESS BOOK OF ALL TIME." DR. KEN BLANCHARD IS FOUNDER OF "THE KEN BLANCHARD COMPANIES", A GLOBAL TRAINING AND CONSULTING COMPANY IN SAN DIEGO, CALIFORNIA. **DR. KEN BLANCHARD HAS PERSONALLY ENDORSED BERNARD AS ONE OF THE MOST EFFECTIVE PUBLIC SPEAKERS HE KNOWS. KEN SAYS, *"BERNARD IS A REAL WINNER!"***

CONTACT BERNARD FOR TRAINING OR KEYNOTE SPEAKING
O. BERNARD SMALLS COMPANIES
P.O. BOX 1359
SUWANEE, GEORGIA, 30024
BUSINESS PHONE: 678. 794.9027
EMAIL: GUNGHOGURU@HOTMAIL.COM
WWW.LULU.COM/BERNARDSMALLS

www.ingramcontent.com/pod-product-compliance
Lightning Source LLC
Chambersburg PA
CBHW032005170526
45157CB00002B/558